Dr. Cass Ingram's

The Cure
is in
the
Cupboard

How to Use Oregano
for Better Health

REVISED EDITION

Knowledge House
Buffalo Grove, Illinois 60089

Printed in the United States of America
First Revised Edition
Ninth Printing 2004

ISBN 0911119744

Disclaimer: This book is not intended as a substitute for medical diagnosis or treatment. Anyone who has a serious disease should consult a physician before initiating any change in treatment or before beginning any new treatment.

For ordering information call (800) 243-5242 (847)-473-4700

Table of Contents

	Introduction	5
Chapter One	**The Natural Antiseptic**	15
Chapter Two	**Medical Uses**	33
Chapter Three	**Everyday Uses**	139
Chapter Four	**Oregano to the Rescue**	147
Chapter Five	**The Hygiene Medicine**	167
Chapter Six	**Conclusion**	175
	Appendices	191
	Bibliography	195
	Index	200

Introduction

Microorganisms are the most predominant of all creatures. Usually, microbes are regarded as an outside force. We don't think of them as being in or on us, but they are and by the billions and even trillions. The fact is the human body is being invaded by a greater number of microbes than can be imagined. It is shocking to learn that within each individual there are a greater number of microbes than all of the cells in the entire body. Put simply, the number of microbes living within our bodies and in our near environment is virtually infinite.

Microbes exert a profound influence upon an individual's health and longevity. Infectious diseases are a major cause of illness, disability, and death in America today. Recent surveys indicate that up to 90% of the visits to doctors' offices are infection related. Infections are certainly the primary cause for hospital visits in infants and children. Virtually everyone can recall at least one hospitalization as a child or teenager because of an infection.

Infectious diseases are the major cause of premature death worldwide, but this is not the case currently in the United States. Degenerative diseases, such as heart disease, diabetes, Alzheimer's disease, and cancer, remain the primary killers. Yet, from the 1600s to the early 1900s the vast majority of deaths in America, other than those occurring from natural causes, were infection related. For instance, in the early 1900s several million Americans died from flu epidemics alone. Certainly, in that era there were other major killers, including cholera, diphtheria, tuberculosis, smallpox, typhus, pertussis, hepatitis, shigella, and amebic dysentery. However, by the 1940s deaths from these diseases had declined dramatically. Various factors, including improved sanitation, nutrition, and the advent of antibiotics, were responsible for the decline. Yet, infections still kill, and the fact is millions of Americans die every year from various infectious diseases.

What seems bizarre is that infectious diseases remain a major cause of death and disability despite the advances of modern medicine. Medicine has simply failed to stem the rising incidence of a variety of microbial diseases, many of which are actually ancient diseases revisited. The latest statistics show that deaths caused by infections have risen from 1980 to 1992 by some 60%. At this rate by the 21st century infectious diseases will rival heart disease and cancer as a primary cause of death.

The astonishing aspect of this infectious epidemic is the impotence of modern medicine in controlling it. Antibiotics have failed to halt the advance of modern-day infectious killers, and there is not a single drug that is a guaranteed cure for any of the major infectious diseases. In fact, drugs, particularly antibiotics, have aggravated the dilemma. This is because the widespread use of antibiotics has created drug-resistant microbes. What happens is that the microbes, due to their propensity for survival, essentially "outsmart" the drugs. They alter their genetics and, thus, become immune to the antibiotic. These "mutant" microbes are a major cause of severe illness in westernized countries.

Because they are genetically altered, mutant microbes are not only able to resist antibiotics, but they are also capable of evading our immune defenses. Incredibly, some bacteria are actually able to digest antibiotics and use a portion of them as fuel. Put simply, they are "genetically intelligent" and therefore extremely difficult to kill.

Infections by mutant microbes are usually severe and often life threatening. Incredibly, according to *Hippocrates* magazine some 130,000 hospitalized patients die every year from antibiotic-resistant microbes in the United States alone. Furthermore, as described by Lappe in *Germs That Won't Die* tens of millions of Americans who are free of serious infections develop them simply by entering a hospital, either as a patient or visitor. These statistics illustrate the massive scope of the mutant microbe epidemic. Surely, uncountable thousands of other individuals suffer severe pain and disability as a result of toxic microbial infections. Incredibly, physicians often literally stand by helplessly—and hopelessly—while the infection takes its course. The point is that every year millions of individuals lose their health or their lives from infections which could be potentially cured, if physicians only knew about the antiseptics of Nature.

Drug resistance is only one of many problems with antibiotics. Allergic reactions to antibiotics are relatively common. The reactions are often sudden and severe. With penicillin alone thousands of deaths occur worldwide from anaphylactic shock. Besides death, significant damage to the immune system and internal organs may result from allergic sensitivity to antibiotics such as penicillin, tetracyclines, sulfa drugs, and cephalosporins. What's more, antibiotics disrupt the balance of microbes in the body. The human body contains untold trillions of germs of various types. These germs live in a sort of competitive balance. When that balance is disrupted, noxious germs may gain a foothold, leading to various disconcerting symptoms as well as frank disease. The point is antibiotics rapidly destroy the healthy bacteria, leading to potential tissue damage by pathogenic bacteria. Plus, antibiotics induce genetic mutants, an effect which is disastrous.

Americans spend billions of dollars every year on antibiotics, either prescription or over-the-counter. Unfortunately, much of this money is wasted. Not only are the antibiotics largely ineffective, but they often aggravate the illnesses. There are several reasons for this negative effect. As mentioned previously antibiotics create the anomalous mutated microbes. The mutants, which are immune to antibiotics, continue to cause infection and are exceedingly difficult to destroy. Antibiotics destroy certain bacteria which perform useful functions, i.e. the friendly bacteria such as Lactobacillus acidophilus and bifidus. These useful bacteria are an aid to the immune system and help prevent infection by noxious microbes. Drug toxicity is another disadvantage arising from the wholesale reliance upon antibiotics. A variety of antibiotics, such as aminoglycosides, erythromycin, and tetracyclines, readily poison the internal organs, leading to measurable damage of vital organs such as the liver, spleen, bone marrow, and kidneys. The fact is antibiotics are a relatively common cause of hepatitis, that is inflammatory damage of the liver. In some cases the damage is so extreme that liver failure and/or death may result. Furthermore, antibiotics exert direct toxic effects upon the immune system and may impair the antimicrobial actions of white blood cells. Although antibiotics are useful in certain circumstances—and may prove lifesaving—the point is they are prescribed excessively, and this leads to a wide range of health disasters.

Unfortunately, antibiotics are often demanded by the public out of fear. They may also be prescribed by doctors because of emotional reasons. For example, parents bring a child suffering from a bad cough and fever to the doctor. The temperature is over 100; the child is cranky and has no appetite. The parents are concerned, rather, scared; the doctor isn't afraid so much of the illness as he/she is of the parents or a potential lawsuit. The parents want something done immediately; the doctor feels obligated to prescribe an antibiotic even though the illness is probably caused by a virus, which is immune to antibiotics. This type of event happens millions of times every day. The fact is tens of millions of antibiotic prescriptions are dispensed erroneously for viral infections each month. Incredibly, rather than a definite medical need, fear of litigation is the motivation for dispensing the prescription. Obviously, the situation is entirely out of control.

Pharmaceutical firms are in a quandary. They cannot create drugs fast enough to keep pace with microbial resistance. They have lost all hope for producing a "magic bullet." Pharmaceutical houses cannot provide medicines capable of stemming the rising tide of drug-resistant infections.

Incredibly, drug companies are for the first time in recent history evaluating the potential of natural substances as well as compounds which enhance immunity as the answer. Yet, in the 1930s natural compounds were the primary substances dispensed for treating infections, and it was the advent of penicillin in the

1940s which displaced them. Before penicillin, itself a natural compound, doctors prescribed a wide range of natural antiseptics, and the list included sulfur, garlic, ginger, goldenseal, echinacea, thyme, camphor, and horseradish. Certainly, drug-like compounds were administered in that era, including silver nitrate, mercury compounds, arsenic compounds, iodine, and phenol. The aforementioned are potentially toxic and have largely been discarded. Other poisons, such as turpentine and petrochemicals, were administered. However, a visit to a museum, antique store, or old pharmacy illustrates the true trend in America before World War II; a review of the labels of old medicine bottles reveals that natural medicines were the mainstay, and this was the case throughout America for over 200 years. In other words, while certain early medicines were poisons or the so-called snake oils containing ingredients like kerosene, turpentine, arsenic, and mercury, the majority were derived from various natural ingredients/herbs such as goldenseal, echinacea, ginger, seneca, balsam, burdock, wintergreen, cinnamon, citronella, coriander, cardamom, cumin, birch bark, cherry bark, clove, thyme, sage, oregano, and dozens of others. All of these herbs possess antibiotic powers.

For untold centuries herbalists and physicians throughout the world used natural substances for treating infections, and microbial resistance was unknown. In the ancient eras as well as relatively recent history natural antibiotics were the only hope for combating microbial infections.

Now too we must rely upon natural medicines to eradicate a panorama of infectious diseases, including drug-resistant infections. Certainly, synthetic antibiotics are unreliable as the cure, plus the side effects are extensive and often severe, whereas, with a few exceptions, natural antibiotics are essentially non-toxic.

Oil of oregano is the premier natural antiseptic. It possesses vast microbial killing powers. Every microbe against which it is tested succumbs to it. Uniquely, there is no tendency for microbial resistance. It is the premier of all natural antiseptics. It is such an effective antiseptic that it cannot be matched either in the synthetic or natural arena in terms of its ability to kill a wide range of microbes.

Oil of oregano is an herbal oil derived from certain species of oregano plants. The medicinal oregano is different from the type usually found in the garden. It is also different than the commercial spice, which is often only a small percentage true oregano.

It is important to realize that wild oregano is not the same as the one found in the spice section of the grocery store or the type found in pizza. However, there are over 30, perhaps as many as 40, species of oregano, and this leads to great confusion in respect to its medicinal actions. In other words oregano as we know of it commercially is not the medicinal variety. Be forewarned that it would be difficult to accrue its curative powers by eating pizza and spaghetti.

Medicinal grade oregano arises from a unique species of plants which grow wild throughout the world. The highest grades are found in the Mediterranean. This "wild" oregano is rich in essential oils, which may be extracted by distillation. The herb is processed by a special type of distillation which has been performed for thousands of years. This "proprietary" distillation procedure ensures minimal alteration of the active ingredients, and thus, the curative powers are entirely preserved. The result is a pale brownish-yellow or amber looking oil possessing a powerful and hot tasting flavor. Its odor is similar to that of camphor. The oil blends readily with fat in which its strong taste and odor is modified. With time oil of oregano turns brown and may eventually develop a dark brown hue. It takes some 200 pounds of the herb to produce 2 pounds of oil. This oil is not only difficult and expensive to produce, but it is entirely unique compared to that found in the more familiar varieties of oregano. Ten thousand pounds of commercial oregano could be distilled and the resultant extract could never achieve the beneficial effects of even a few ounces of wild oil of oregano.

The oregano used in food, such as that found in spaghetti sauce and pizza, which is also the type that may be purchased at the spice counter, isn't even oregano. It is marjoram and is known as sweet marjoram. It is regarded as sweet, because its flavor is rather pleasant and is utterly mild compared to the true oregano. Marjoram, not oregano, is commonly the spice which is added to pizzas. The herb and oil are utilized by food processors to flavor everything from meats and sauces to alcoholic beverages and soft drinks. Oil of marjoram is used as a fragrance for soaps, detergents, and cosmetics and is also an ingredient of perfumes. Furthermore, some of the common spice isn't even marjoram let alone oregano. For instance, virtually all of the so-called oregano available on the West Coast is instead an oregano-like plant from Mexico. This species is entirely unrelated botanically to either oregano or marjoram. It merely tastes similar to oregano and is actually Mexican sage.

Because of these discrepancies, it is crucial to realize just what the terms oil of oregano, crushed wild oregano, and oregano spice mean in reference to this book. These terms define entirely different substances than the commercially available spices and plants. In other words, whatever the supermarket has on its shelves or whatever the health food purveyor might provide, it isn't medicinal grade oregano: period. Such products will not and cannot exhibit the curative effects described in this book. The only guaranteed wild medicinal grade oregano spice and oil available is made by North American Herb and Spice Company under the trade names *Oregamax* and *Oreganol.* These compounds are derived from true oregano species. Only these can be relied upon to possess the various health advancing attributes that are to be expected of the true herb.

Infections are merely one of a panorama of uses for oil of oregano. This profound substance exerts valuable anti-inflammatory actions. Furthermore, it is an antioxidant. It has an anti-venom action and is capable of neutralizing the venom of a wide range of organisms, including spiders, scorpions, bees, ants, and snakes. Oregano oil is a natural anesthetic, and thus, it is invaluable in the treatment of various painful lesions and pain disorders. It is also a mucolytic, which means it helps thin and mobilize mucus, and this function makes it useful for lung disorders. It is an antitussive agent, meaning it halts cough and eases spasticity of the lung tubules. Additionally, oil of oregano possesses antispasmodic powers, meaning it obliterates tightness and spasms of the muscles.

Despite the multitude of its use, the greatest attribute of the oil is a result of its antimicrobial powers. Oil of oregano holds supremacy as Nature's most powerful and versatile antiseptic.

Chapter One **The Natural Antiseptic**

No one in America seems to know a great deal about oil of oregano, although everyone is familiar with the pizza spice. The plant from which oil of oregano is derived is different than the oregano with which we are familiar. It is a substance derived from a special species of wild oregano, which is botanically and chemically distinct compared to commercial oregano.

All species of true oregano belong to the mint family. However, there are dozens of species plus a variety of subspecies. Of the 60-plus species of oregano or oregano-like plants, relatively few possess significant medicinal powers.

Three products are discussed in this book: oil of oregano, oregano juice, and crushed wild oregano. The crushed wild oregano consists of the entire herb, which is in its original natural state. The only processing it undergoes is that it is sun-dried. Oil of oregano is the essential oil of the wild oregano plant, which is produced by steam distillation. Oregano essence is the water soluble extract of wild oregano, which is also produced by steam distillation. Oil of oregano, the essence (or juice), and the crushed herb are strictly products of Nature, substances which exhibit curative powers superseding anything previously known in America as well as the rest of the Western world.

Oil of oregano is produced by an old-fashioned distillation process, which preserves the curative powers of the active ingredients. Minimal heat is used in processing, and the resultant product is entirely unrefined. That is, it remains in its original state. The oil is extracted from the crushed dried leaves and flowers of various species of oregano, which grow wild on the hillsides, mountains, and in the forests of various regions throughout the world. Only certain species of oregano qualify for making the oil, and these species are difficult to obtain.

Oil of oregano's antiseptic powers are immense. Nothing else in Nature can match it, and pharmaceutical drugs are weaklings compared to it. Singlehandedly, it can kill and/or block the growth of virtually any fungus. It destroys viruses and parasites. Furthermore, it inhibits the growth of as well as destroys the majority of bacteria, something that prescription antibiotics often fail to accomplish. According to the latest research (2001) it even destroys super-germs, that is the ones which are antibiotic-resistant. Plus, there is no evidence of bacterial resistance, a property unheard of in today's phamaceuticals.

Researchers have tested a variety of spices for purported antibiotic activity. This research was performed in the hope of finding spices that could halt or impede the spoilage of food. Of all spices tested oregano was the only one to exhibit significant antifungal and antibacterial activity. This ability to destroy both bacteria and fungi makes oregano oil unique in the spice kingdom. Finding it difficult to believe that a natural substance could be this powerful, the federal government also tested oil of oregano. In an attempt to prove it didn't work they found the opposite: oil of oregano killed every germ against which it was tested. Nine pathogens succumbed, including salmonella, E. coli, listeria, staph, pseudomonas, and molds.

Oil of oregano's antiviral properties are significant. Siddiqui, publishing in *Medical Science Research,* proved that the oil completely destroys a wide range of viruses, including the herpes virus. Parasites also fall prey to oil of oregano, and virtually all species, including worms, amoebas, and protozoans, succumb to its killing powers.

Researchers publishing in the *International Journal of Food Microbiology* (1988) evaluated the antiseptic powers of a number of spices. The method used was to grow various organisms in petri dishes in order to halt microbial growth by adding various spices. Of all the spices tested, which included coriander, dill, bay leaf, spearmint, basil, and mustard, oregano possessed the most significant microbial killing ability. The fact is all other spices were regarded as entirely impotent as antiseptics.

In America essential oil of oregano, the type made from the medicinal plant, has been entirely unavailable since the early 1900s, that is until recently (1996). While certain herbal catalogues may list products such as marjoram oil, wild oregano oil, Origanum vulgare oil, or oil of oregano, the problem is that the commercially available oil is almost exclusively thyme oil and/or marjoram oil and is erroneously labeled as oregano oil. The thyme oil is usually produced from a non-oregano plant, *Thymus capitus.* It is not oregano oil nor does it possess its medicinal attributes. In fact, thyme oil, despite being derived from an edible herb, may be toxic. The reason it is called oregano oil is that the Spanish species of thyme from which the oil is distilled is known as "Spanish oregano." According to Julia

Lawless, who writes about Spanish oregano in her book *The Encyclopedia of Essential Oils,* "Although this herb is strictly a thyme, it serves as the source for most so-called oregano oil." The point is the oil extracted from Spanish oregano and that extracted from true medicinal oregano are entirely different, which is understandable, since they are different species. For instance, thyme oil contains large amounts of *thymol*, a compound exhibiting significant toxicity, whereas the primary component of oregano oil is *carvacrol*. Another drawback is the fact that commercial thyme oil is usually adulterated and may contain potentially toxic additives. Marjoram oil is another type of oil erroneously labeled as oregano oil, and Lawless notes that a small percentage of commercial oil is derived from it. Thus, virtually none of the commercially available oil is truly of the oregano species. Furthermore, commercial thyme and marjoram oil are often heavily refined, and this increases the toxicity while reducing effectiveness. Thus, such oils cannot be deemed safe for internal use in any amount and must even be used externally with caution.

Prior to the publication of this book the data available on the health benefits of oregano spice and its essential oil was minimal. Nor were these substances readily available for human consumption. It took several years to discover this unique oil, which exhibits a plethora of curative effects. Another year was required to procure it and yet another to investigate its attributes. This is important to understand, because the nutrition industry is fraught with a tendency to copy any new product. The industry is devoid of creativity or research capacity of its own. Rather, the tendency is to merely copy any new idea or product if it is deemed trendy or lucrative.

Unfortunately, the usual result is the creation of a hastily designed, inferior product sold through aggressive marketing. As a result of this greed no one wins, and most importantly, the consumer is the ultimate loser. Regarding oregano oil **beware of cheap and possibly dangerous imitations.**

Alas, the public is dependent upon whether or not a company is ethical or if vested interests lead to a distortion of the facts. For instance, recently a one-sided article about an obesity drug in the *New England Journal of Medicine* was relinquished, because the authors had commercial connections with the maker of the drug.

Don't administer oil of oregano, either externally or especially internally, unless there is certainty that it is the correct substance. In any event, the oil should not be consumed in large amounts internally. Never consume commercial essential oils of any type internally. The advice contained in this book applies only to the use of pure, unprocessed oil of oregano derived from the various true oregano species. The intent is to help the individual in health improvement; in other words, the Hippocratic Oath of "above all, do no harm" is the policy. Thyme oil or other oils which are heavily refined should not be administered internally nor should, for that matter, any essential oil unless it has been proven to be free of adulterants or safe to use. A number of essential oils possess significant toxicity, and this is largely the result of how they are prepared and the fact that they are adulterated.

The fact is the majority of commercially available essential oils are unfit for human consumption in any amount; they can only be applied topically. Tea tree oil is one of the most commonly utilized essential oils. Applied topically, it is entirely safe and quite versatile, although allergic reactions may occur. Taken internally, it is toxic and may cause liver and kidney damage—perhaps death. Researchers in Australia found that in high doses tea tree oil caused respiratory failure and coma, an indication that it is highly toxic to the internal organs, particularly the brain.

The essential oils which are the safest to consume are those made from food grade herbs. Certain herbs are foods, while others are only used as medicines. For instance, oregano is a food, and thus, its oil is much less toxic than oils from inedible, non-food plants such as Melaluca and pennyroyal. The latter is so toxic that its ingestion may lead to death. British pharmacopoeias note that pennyroyal is useful for intestinal gas, virus infections, and gout. Even so, it would be precarious to advise anyone to ingest even a drop of commercial pennyroyal oil. The fact is pennyroyal is an inedible weed. In contrast, common herbs and spices such as cinnamon, cloves, garlic, onion, coriander, oregano, cardamom, and mint are edible, and so are their oils. This doesn't mean edible oils should be consumed with impunity. On the contrary, only small to moderate amounts of such herbal oils have been deemed safe, and only those which are listed on the FDA's GRAS list (i.e. Generally Regarded as Safe) should be consumed. Oil of oregano is one such oil.

Although we don't think about it, we consume essential oils every day. Every time we use mint or cinnamon-flavored gum or candy, we are consuming essential oils. Toothpaste and soft drinks are flavored with mint or cinnamon oil. Many "Italian" sauces are flavored with oil of marjoram and/or oil of oregano. Onion and garlic oils are instilled in many processed foods, as is cayenne oil. Oil of dill is added to pickles; it's not just the herbs at the bottom of the jar that are responsible for their flavor. Dill oil is also used in soft drinks and alcoholic beverages. While you may have never eaten the famous French herb chervil, you have probably consumed the essential oil unknowingly, as it is a common additive in processed meats, alcoholic beverages, and soft drinks. Who would believe that the American diet includes consuming parts of trees? Birch oil, which is distilled from the bark and twigs of the common birch tree, is used extensively by food processors and is a major flavoring for root beer.

The point is that in minute quantities essential oils are safe—and this is even true of certain non-food plants like birch. However, the safest oils are derived from foods such as garlic, onion, chervil, dill, cinnamon, cloves, cardamom, cumin, fennel, and oregano, and we consume minute quantities of these oils within the foods we eat every day.

The Killing Power

Oil of oregano, like all essential oils, contains a wide range of substances. No one knows for sure what is the exact nature of all of the ingredients. However, one well studied compound that predominates in the oil is a substance known as *carvacrol*, a type of phenol. Carvacrol is found in only a few herbs, notably oregano and savory, and oregano's rich content of this antiseptic is one reason it is so unique. Phenols are potent antiseptics. In fact, synthetic phenol, known also as carbolic acid, was for much of the 20th century used as the standard by which all other antiseptics were measured. As late as the 1950s carbolic acid was the primary antiseptic used for sterilizing instruments prior to surgery and was the main antiseptic used in hospitals. Oregano's phenol, carvacrol, is significantly more potent than the synthetic variety. Furthermore, oil of oregano contains small amounts (less than 2%) of yet another phenolic compound known as *thymol*, a compound similar to that found in thyme oil. These small amounts of thymol are completely safe for human consumption. Carvacrol and thymol work synergistically. This means oil of oregano packs a double punch in antiseptic power and explains why it is infinitely more potent than commercial phenol in microbial killing power.

It is to be expected that the naturally occurring phenols found in oil of oregano, such as carvacrol and thymol, are more potent than the synthetic type. Nature, the master of synthesis, has produced oil of oregano as a mixture of synergistic chemicals, each possessing antibiotic activity. Some of the compounds are so unique that they have yet to be identified let alone synthesized. The main component, carvacrol, has never been precisely reproduced. Phenol has been synthesized, but it cannot match the antiseptic strength of carvacrol. Yet, it is the continuity of the oil, that is the unprocessed complete oil, that accounts for its unmatched antimicrobial actions. The fact is oil of oregano contains over 50 compounds which possess antimicrobial actions, although carvacrol and thymol are the primary active ingredients.

Relatively few species of oregano contain rich supplies of carvacrol. These are the types used by the North American Herb and Spice Company. As determined by Akgul and Kivanc,

The Natural Antiseptic 23

publishing in the *International Journal of Food Microbiology*, carvacrol is one of the most potent of all known natural antiseptics and is the lead ingredient accounting for oregano's antiseptic actions. Baser, Dean of Pharmacology at Andalou University, notes that there is great confusion in the nomenclature of oregano species and that many of these species are low in the active ingredient. However, if the herb is correctly sourced and is harvested from the proper species, up to seventy percent of the oil fraction consists of carvacrol. For a list of the medicinal compounds found in oil of oregano see Appendix B.

Oil of oregano has been evaluated thoroughly in the test tube regarding its antiseptic powers. As described by Sarer and colleagues in *Essential Oils and Aromatic Plants,* extracts of a rather mild species showed "remarkable effects" against a wide range of microbes. The authors note how the oil and its derivatives completely inhibited the growth of various fungi which attack the skin (i.e. the dermatophytes), while strongly inhibiting the growth of Candida albicans. A significant destruction was also observed against certain bacteria, notably staph, strep, and E. coli. Even the growth of Pseudomonas, which is notoriously difficult to destroy, was significantly inhibited, a feat rarely accomplished by even the most potent synthetic drugs. Yet more impressive is research published in the *International Journal of Food Microbiology* describing the antiseptic powers of wild mountain oregano. The authors observed a complete inhibition in the growth of all fungi tested with oregano oil. What was so astounding was the fact that these effects were noted in minute concentrations. Incredibly, a mere 1% solution induced complete destruction of nine species of fungi. Furthermore, the researchers tested an isolate of the oil; they used carvacrol alone. Astonishingly, a solution of it amounting to a mere one quarter of one percent was sufficient to inhibit the growth of all fungi tested. Using the pure oil, Tantaoui-Elaraki and Beraoud, publishing in the *Journal of Environmental Pathology, Toxicology, and Oncology*, observed a potent antiseptic effect against fungi in a mere one tenth of a percent concentration. Here is how the research was performed: fungal organisms are seeded into a growing medium on a petri dish. A certain amount of growth is expected. When oil of oregano was added to the medium, growth was halted. In some instances no fungal growth whatsoever was seen on the petri dish, meaning that the oil halted fungal growth 100%. In more common terms this means that oil of oregano completely destroyed the fungi. These observations elevate oil of oregano to an unprecedented status: that of the most potent naturally occurring antifungal agent known.

Fungal Infection: the Bane of Humanity

Fungal infection is a major cause of disease in the Western world. Recently, the important role of fungal organisms in the causation of illness has become evident, although for decades the medical profession has ignored their crucial role.

A fungus is defined as a saprophyte, meaning it lives off of dead or dying tissue. Fungi, the plural of fungus, thrive wherever there is dead or decaying matter. Yet, fungi are common inhabitants of living beings, although they tend to proliferate when the organism is diseased. This "living off the dead" attribute of fungi explains why they commonly infect the skin. The skin is constantly shedding layers of dead cells, and these cells are an ideal medium for a fungal feast.

After defining these organisms it seems rather ominous that everyone has fungi living within their bodies. In fact, there are billions of them living within each of us. Researchers note that they may account for up to 3% of the normal microbe count within the body. To give you an idea of how many organisms this would amount to, there are a greater number of microbes in the human body than there are actual cells, and there are some 70 trillion cells in each of our bodies. The microbes live on us everywhere; on the skin, in the mouth, along the intestines, and throughout the genitourinary tract. While it may be incorrect to state that we cannot live without them, there is no doubt that we have little choice but to live with them. We don't have to worry about killing them all, because under normal circumstances they do little or no harm. Yet, the objective is to live with the various microbes within us in a balance, a sort of peaceful coexistence, because, if they overpopulate, they can cause extensive disease, disability, and even death.

Obviously, since fungi thrive on diseased tissue, the existence of a fungal or yeast infection is a sign of compromised health. In a strong, healthy body it would be difficult for such an infection to gain a foothold. However, once they become established within the body, fungi and yeasts are notoriously difficult to destroy. Even so, these stubborn organisms are no match for oil of oregano. This essential oil is capable of destroying fungi wherever they abound. This broadens the usage of the compound to infinity. Think of the immense value to be derived. Whether the problem is a mold infestation in the shower or basement or a bad case of athlete's foot, oregano oil will come to the rescue. Furthermore, it is a valuable treatment for a wide range of fungal infections occurring within the body.

Millions of Americans are afflicted with fungal infections, whether internal or external. Although they were once regarded as rare, medical authorities note that fungal infections have reached epidemic proportions and that they are rising in incidence by as much as 25% per year. The elderly and very young are particularly vulnerable, as are surgical and/or hospitalized patients. However, because of the lifestyle of Americans virtually everyone is a candidate for infection.

Americans are the most fungally infested people in the world. This is directly related to the type of diet followed in America. Fungi feed primarily upon one substance: sugar. The American diet is highest in sugar of any nation, with the average American consumption amounting to some 150 pounds per person per year. This is an incredibly large quantity of sugar. Visualize this quantity. If you are average, you consume a minimum of one ten pound bag of sugar per month (the last month, December, equals a thirty pound bag). If you are a major sweet/sugar eater, you consume perhaps as much as a twenty pound bag per month. That amount of sugar is enough to readily disable the body, physically and mentally. Even if you are a modest sweet/sugar eater, you consume a five pound bag of pure, white, nutrient-free sugar per month. Besides depleting the body of critical nutrients, sugar disrupts metabolism and damages the glands. It also represses the immune system. Furthermore, sugar feeds fungi, and this leads to the overgrowth of various fungal organisms and yeasts within the body as well as on the skin, nails, and scalp. A recent study determined that as little as a teaspoon or two daily was enough to stimulate fungal growth.

Alcohol is yet another stimulant for fungal growth. This is because alcohol depresses immunity by depleting nutrients. Furthermore, alcohol is toxic to the immune system. Even a couple of drinks every day or every other day is enough to induce destruction of both immune cells and immune glands such as the lymph nodes, spleen, and, particularly, the bone marrow. The result is that less immune cells are available to combat microbes. Think again before using alcohol as a heart disease cure. While it may lower cholesterol levels, the negative effects are not worth enduring. Researchers have thoroughly documented how the regular use of alcohol damages white blood cells, corrodes the liver, oxidizes the spleen, poisons the bone marrow, and insults the brain, plus the heart is far from immune to it. Alcohol consumption is the number one cause of high blood pressure, and it causes its own type of heart disease: cardiomyopathy.

Other drugs which damage the internal organs and weaken immunity include antibiotics, birth control pills, chemotherapeutic agents, anti-inflammatory drugs, and radiation. In particular, the latter causes extensive bone marrow damage and leaves the individual highly vulnerable for the development of opportunistic infections.

Antibiotics are perhaps the major factor in the cause of fungal infestation and are certainly the leading cause of acute fungal infections of the vagina, intestines, and mouth. It is not just the prescriptions which are responsible; residues of antibiotics are found in food, particularly meat products, frozen fish, milk, and eggs. Antibiotics destroy the helpful bacteria, organisms which inhibit the growth of fungi. Thus, antibiotics kill microbes indiscriminately. Once the inhibitory or helpful bacteria are eliminated the fungi grow throughout the body fulminately.

Birth control pills greatly enhance fungal growth. Anyone who has regularly taken birth control pills for several years is vulnerable for fungal overgrowth. The estrogens in these pills cause fungi to flourish, particularly Candida albicans.

Cortisone greatly accelerates fungal growth. If cortisone is consumed for prolonged periods, fungal infestation is assured. This is particularly true of prednisone. This drug is the most potent type of cortisone. It enhances fungal growth by repressing the function of the adrenal glands, an organ system responsible for enhancing immune defenses against fungi. Furthermore, cortisone destroys lymphocytes, the type of white blood cell required for fighting fungal infections. The fact is long term consumption of cortisone leads to atrophy, that is shrinkage, of the lymph glands, a rather disastrous side effect. Topical use also increases the risk for fungal infection.

There are thousands of species of fungi, and only a few of these normally infect humans. However, individuals are becoming infested with an ever increasing variety of molds, yeasts, and fungi; organisms previously deemed impotent are now being diagnosed as pathogens. This illustrates the immense vulnerability of individuals on a high sugar diet, as well as alcoholics, for the development of fungal infections. Let's face it, fungi love sugar, and whether that sugar is found in fruit, human blood, or the forest floor, it will feed fungal growth. The fact is the Western diet, rich in sugar and processed starches, breeds fungal infection.

If fungal organisms disrupt the normal microbial balance within the body by overpopulating, they can cause extensive disease. One of the greatest concerns with fungal infections is the fact that all pathogenic, that is toxic, fungi induce immune suppression. It makes sense that they would attempt to disrupt immune defenses; obviously, once they gain a foothold they attempt to retain their advances. Thus, they create an incredibly sophisticated array of defense mechanisms which are, in a sense, more offensive than defensive. Many theories have been proposed to explain why yeast/fungal infections result in diminished immunity. Some researchers believe that this is due to the liberation of fungal toxins, which poison the immune system. Others note that fungi alter the structure of their cell walls to evade destruction by white blood cells. Whatever the mechanism is, the ultimate result is that fungi disable the immune system's ability to destroy them and, thus, their preservation is assured.

If the fungi are given free reign as a result of neutralized immunity, they can cause extensive disease. Pathogenic fungi are highly invasive and are capable of infesting virtually any tissue and organ, including the skin, lungs, liver, spleen, thymus, adrenal glands, intestines, pancreas, bladder, kidneys, ovaries, prostate, uterus, esophagus, rectum, and even the brain. Despite the output of the potent antibiotic hydrochloric acid, fungi may even invade the stomach. The latter illustrates the aggressive, invasive and survival powers of these organisms. A more glaring example of the unbridled power of fungi is the fact that when nuclear bombs were first tested in the 1940s and 50s various microbes were subjected to the fallout. The one organism which readily survived was a fungus/yeast: Candida albicans. The epitome of "genetic engineering," this yeast mutated to avoid the toxicity of nuclear irradiation. With an organism so indestructible can we expect an unassisted immune system to defeat it? Our immune systems are powerful, but they may be incapable of mustering sufficient strength to routinely defeat fungi, since they are greater survivalists than the human race itself and are continuously striving to evade the immune or chemical assaults leveled against them. What's more, the fungi are constantly mutating, making it difficult for the immune system to destroy them.

This is what makes wild oil of oregano such a boon. For the first time in their prolific existence fungi have met their match. Oil of oregano outright destroys all varieties of fungi and yeasts, regardless of where they reside. Even the mutants succumb to its aggressive antiseptic powers. The fact is fungi have nowhere to hide. If they are on the skin, it destroys them. If they are within the body, it destroys them. If they are on inanimate objects, it decimates them. If they are in the air, it neutralizes them. If you have a serious fungal infection, don't give up hope. Oil of wild oregano may save your life.

Chapter Two   **Medical Uses**

The medical uses of oil of oregano are vast. To appreciate how to utilize it and what conditions it is used for it is important to review the history, botany, and chemistry of the oregano plant.

The name oregano is derived from a Grecian word meaning "joy of the mountains," seemingly an allusion to the pleasing effect this plant gave to the Greeks as it grew on their hillsides and mountains. However, the definition may have been more physiological than spiritual; the Greeks utilized this herb extensively as a medicine. It is perhaps one of the reasons their civilization was so powerful, mentally and physically. Oregano was a favorite prescription of ancient Grecian physicians. Conditions treated included trauma, open wounds, headaches, lung disorders, including asthma, seizures, venomous bites, and congestive heart failure. They even used it for reversing narcotic poisoning. Furthermore, the ancients regarded it as a definitive cure for poisoning by dangerous plants, like poison hemlock.

During the Middle Ages Islamic doctors used oregano spice as well as the essential oil as a germ killer. In the open markets in 9th century Baghdad powdered wild oregano was sprinkled on produce to keep it fresh, one historian noting that vegetables stayed unspoiled for up to two weeks, without refrigeration. In

Medieval Europe bunches of wild oregano were hung over milk pails to prevent microbial growth.

Over the centuries oregano has been highly touted as a remedy for a wide range of lung conditions, including asthma, pneumonia, bronchitis, sinusitis, and cough. In his 17th century manuscript Britain's Gerard described how oregano was the ideal remedy for head colds.

Herbalists in the Western world are increasingly relying upon the powers of wild oregano. They use it externally for aching joints or muscles, headaches, arthritis, toothaches, and sore gums. As inhalation therapy it is used for a wide range of lung conditions. Internally, they use it for cleansing the intestines of noxious germs as well as for acute infections, like sore throats, tonsillitis, colds, and flu. In the Orient oregano is used to treat fever, vomiting, diarrhea, skin rashes, and itchy skin.

The oregano plant is rather unique in the herbal kingdom, because it possesses a strong, peculiar odor and a warm almost bitter taste. In an herbal garden the odor usually overpowers that of all other plants. These properties are largely preserved even in the dry herb. The leaves of the oregano plant are filled with oil, which may be seen as vesicles upon the leaves when they are held up to light. This heavy oil content is primarily found in wild oregano leaves. Farm-raised or garden-grown oregano leaves are devoid of the oil vesicles. The oil is readily preserved when the leaves are dried and it keeps for prolonged periods without becoming rancid. Once the herb is dried, the oil, which accounts for about two percent of the dry weight, may be readily extracted via distillation.

For thousands of years oregano has been extensively consumed as a food in the Mediterranean, Middle East, and also Eastern

Europe. While the Europeans use it on salads, people in the Middle East put food on their oregano; in other words, they eat it virtually as a staple, like we might eat wheat. A dish made in Egypt, Lebanon, and Syria contains a crust of crushed oregano immersed in olive oil spread upon pita bread. Incredibly, this oregano crust may be nearly as thick as the bread itself. Thus, obviously the primitives have consistently valued it nutritionally. This brings up the crucial issue of just what is in oregano spice and its oil. Let's begin by reviewing the food value of this fascinating substance.

Nutritional Value

Oregano is a spice which grows wild on rocky or calcium-rich soils. Thus, this potent spice thrives on mineral-rich earth. Indeed, a review of its nutritional status illustrates that this is precisely the case.

Wild oregano is a veritable natural mineral treasure trove, containing a density of minerals that would rival, in fact, supersede, any food. The minerals it contains are perhaps too numerous to mention, however, the major ones include calcium, magnesium, iron, phosphorus, copper, zinc, boron, potassium, and manganese. Overall, its density of minerals makes it one of the richest plant sources of trace minerals known. Incredibly, it contains a whopping 1600 mg-plus of calcium per 100 grams, making it richer in this mineral than the traditional sources. Ounce for ounce oregano is richer in calcium than cheese, dark green vegetables, salmon, sardines, and, yes, milk. The fact is oregano contains more than twice the calcium content of American cheese and, unbelievably, some 16 times the calcium of milk. Furthermore, dark green leafy vegetables, the highly touted vegetarian source for calcium, cannot even compare to the immense calcium density of oregano. Thus, a wild oregano supplement may be used as a virtual natural calcium and magnesium pill.

Despite the enormity of its calcium content its iron reservoir is even more impressive. Incredibly, oregano contains approximately 50 mg of iron per 100 grams. This is an incredibly large amount of organic iron. Ensminger lists it as one of the top eight sources, well ahead of traditional sources such as liver, molasses, red meat, and eggs. For instance, oregano is nearly three times as high in iron as blackstrap molasses. It is likely that certain species, such as the type used in Oregamax, are significantly higher in iron content, making oregano spice, short of dried parsley, the top commercially available source of naturally occurring iron.

Some types of iron are not good for the body. Researchers have shown that synthetic iron, such as the type found in multiple vitamins, iron pills, and fortified food, can be toxic. This is particularly true for males and postmenopausal females. Natural iron, as occurs in plant life, is nontoxic and may be consumed by men and women regardless of age.

Oregano contains a relatively large amount of magnesium, and this is ideal, since magnesium aids in calcium metabolism. It is one of the top 20 commercially available sources of this valuable trace mineral, containing some 280 mg per 100 grams. This means oregano is richer in magnesium than highly touted food sources such as cashews, peanuts, molasses, whole grains, beet greens, and spinach. Magnesium is crucial for a wide range of functions, including bone formation and protein synthesis.

The zinc content is incredibly high. Oregano contains about 4 mg per 100 grams, making it a richer source of this mineral than sardines, salmon, cheese, peanut butter, and whole grains. Current research indicates that as many as 80% of Americans fail to get sufficient zinc in the diet. As a result, zinc deficiency is rampant.

Copper is another trace mineral found in oregano in unusually large amounts. Depending upon the batch, oregano contains as much as 1 mg of copper per 100 grams. This is an impressive amount. Copper is a difficult mineral to procure in the food chain. The only commonly consumed sources listed in Ensminger's *Foods and Nutrition Encyclopedia* that equal or supersede oregano are oysters (by far the richest natural source), liver, molasses, cocoa powder, black pepper, Brazil nuts, sunflower seeds, olives, walnuts, almonds, pecans, and whole wheat. The copper in whole wheat is difficult to absorb, but the type found in oregano is readily absorbed.

Like many other spices oregano contains a considerable amount of potassium. According to the USDA oregano offers nearly 1700 mg of potassium per 100 grams, which places it well above many of the commonly touted sources, including orange juice, bananas, apricots, dates, and dark green leafy vegetables. It is important to note that the type of potassium found in oregano is efficiently absorbed, and, thus, this herb may be utilized as a non-toxic potassium supplement. Thus, it becomes obvious that wild oregano is a virtual herbal multiple-mineral supplement.

The vitamin content of oregano has yet to be thoroughly elucidated. However, according to Taintu's *Spices and Seasonings* oregano contains over 6 mg of niacin per 100 grams. This means that oregano has a niacin content equal to that of beef, commercial rice, and whole wheat. Other vitamins found in oregano include beta carotene, vitamin C, vitamin K, riboflavin, and thiamine.

Oregano spice from the various true oregano species is a rich source of pigments. These pigments are known as flavonoids. Flavonoids are potent compounds, with significant medicinal properties. Wild oregano is far richer in powerful flavonoids than commercial or farm-raised types. The pigments/flavonoids possess antioxidant, anti-inflammatory, and anti-pain properties. Certain of the oregano flavonoids are thought to fight cancer or even help the body kill cancer cells.

The Chemistry of Oregano Oil

Oil of oregano consists of hundreds of compounds, some of which are known scientifically and others of which are unknown. However, the majority of its unique compounds can be divided into three categories:

a) *Phenols:* these are complex chemicals noted chemically by possessing an aromatic hydrocarbon ring. Phenols are found in a wide range of plants. Popularly known as carbolic acid, synthetic phenol is derived through distillation of coal tar, the latter being a residue resulting from the petrochemical processing of coal. The main naturally occurring phenols in oregano oil are carvacrol and thymol. Both are potent natural antiseptics. Like all phenols they exert their actions through a caustic effect upon tissues. This caustic nature explains oregano's destructive actions against microbes as well as cancer cells. Phenols also possess significant antioxidant activity.

b) *Terpenes:* these are long chain hydrocarbons which are found in a wide variety of plant oils. Short chain hydrocarbons are exceedingly common in nature, but the majority have no therapeutic use. An example is benzene, a gasoline component, which has six carbons in its molecule. In contrast, terpenes contain at least 10 carbon atoms, and this long chain is responsible for their aggressive chemical properties. Terpenes are highly soluble in fatty substances. In other words, they aggressively penetrate into fats, and that includes the fatty membranes of living cells. This is why terpene rich oils make excellent massage oils.

Terpenes are the primary active ingredients of citrus oils. For instance, limonene is a potent antiviral terpene found in lemon oil. Terpenes are potent antiseptic, antiviral, and anti-inflammatory agents. Certain terpenes act as natural anesthetics, which means they are capable of halting pain. Oil of oregano contains dozens of terpenes, including pinene (the same type as is found in pine needles), bisabolene, caryophyllene, cymene, and terpinene.

c) *Alcohols:* not all alcohols are alike. This chemical category covers a massive range of compounds. While ethyl alcohol has limited medicinal actions, nature creates a wide array of large alcohol molecules which possess significant medicinal properties while exhibiting minimal or no toxicity.

The types of alcohols found in oregano oil are devoid of intoxicating effects; they are called long chain alcohols and are useful medicines. Long chain alcohols are relatively effective antiseptics and are particularly noted for their antiviral powers. Oregano's long chain alcohols include linalol and bonreol.

d) *esters:* Nature forms a variety of chemicals through brilliantly designed synthetic reactions, and one group of these impressive chemicals is the esters. Esters found in large quantities in oregano oil include geranyl acetate and linalyl acetate. These substances are also found in sage and lavender oils. Esters are noted for their potent antifungal powers. They also possess a mild sedative or relaxing effect and enhance blood flow throughout the body.

Oregano, a Potent Antioxidant?

As early as the 1940s it was discovered that spices acted as preservatives when added to foods and food oils. Food chemists studying baked goods noticed that certain spices prevented the fat used in bakery from turning rancid. Later, it was determined that the primary agents responsible in these spices were phenolic compounds, and these are the primary chemicals found in oil of oregano. Later research determined that other compounds in oregano, notably labiatic and p-hydroxyhydrocaffeic acid, accounted for its antioxidant powers.

French researchers were intrigued by the potential antioxidant capacity of spices of the mint family, including oregano. The researchers measured the ability of the plants to halt free radical production. They noted that oregano possesses "significant antioxidant activities" and that this is largely due to its content of two antioxidant chemicals: rosmarinic and hydroxycinnamic acids.

The antioxidant powers of a substance are a measurement of its ability to preserve items, whether it be the cells in the human body or the food we eat. Food chemists were intrigued by the potential applications for oregano as a food preservative. Thus, they added oregano to a number of foods to see if the shelf life could be extended. When tested against several other spices oregano was determined to be superior to all others as a preservative for creamy based foods such as mayonnaise and salad dressings. In 1998 the U.S. government tested the preservative powers of oil of oregano. Comparing to other spice oils they found that oil of oregano was the most effective one in keeping food from spoiling. Incredibly, after coating it with an oregano oil marinade researchers kept fresh tuna fish from spoiling for nearly six weeks. What's more, the oregano oil killed nine different pathogens responsible for spoiling food, including E. coli, salmonella, listeria, staph, and mold. The researchers concluded that oregano oil was far more effective at preventing food spoilage and halting microbial growth than the mere ground spice.

Now we know what is in oil of oregano and oregano spice as well as perhaps how it works on or in the body. Let's review how it can be used in specific diseases.

Acne

Acne is a skin infection afflicting primarily adolescents and teenagers. Perhaps there is nothing more feared by a teenager—even a principal's discipline—than a bad case of acne. Teenagers do everything in their power to cleanse, medicate, or cover the lesions, usually to no avail. Interestingly, only rarely will a teenager alter his/her diet in order to resolve it, which is certainly a major factor in this illness.

No one knows for sure precisely what causes acne. The most popular theory is that it is an infectious disease. Specifically, the sebaceous glands, the tiny oil secreting glands found in great numbers on the face, upper back, and chest, become infected by various microbes, particularly bacteria. The primary microbial culprits include staph, strep, and Candida albicans. However, certainly hormonal issues are involved, since acne develops at a time when hormone levels are changing dramatically. An imbalance in steroids, such as testosterone, estrogen, progesterone, and adrenal steroids, as well as thyroid hormones, may precipitate or aggravate the condition, particularly in adolescents. Severe acne may warn of sluggish thyroid function, that is hypothyroidism, which is manifested by a variety of symptoms, including low energy, poor concentration, delayed development, learning impairment, and obesity. However, as mentioned previously diet is a major factor. According to a variety of scientific studies certain foods may aggravate acne, including citrus fruit, chocolate, deep fried foods, nuts, and pork. Processed foods and various food additives are the primary culprits. Certain ubiquitous components of processed foods, notably refined vegetable oils, hydrogenated oils, nitrates, sugar, caffeine, food dyes, sulfites, and cocoa, greatly aggravate acne and may act as the primary cause. Many of these foods aggravate or cause acne by disrupting hormone metabolism.

Whatever are the aggravating factors, the end result is infection and/or inflammation of the sebaceous ducts, glands, hair follicles, and surrounding skin. Bacteria, fungi, parasites, and even mites may be involved.

The pH of the skin has been correlated with the vulnerability in developing acne. Acidic pH is protective, while an alkaline pH encourages microbial growth, especially fungal growth. The normal pH of the skin is about 5.0, which is quite acidic. Hormonal changes in teenagers may alter the normally protective acidic pH of the skin towards alkalinity, which increases the risk for the growth of unwanted microbes. Commercial soaps, which are lye-based, that is alkaline, are also a factor. Be sure soaps used on the face are either acidic in pH or neutral.

Oil of oregano is an effective cure for acne. It may be applied directly upon the lesions and can also be added to soaps or cleansers. The oil possesses potent anti-inflammatory and antibiotic actions directed against the microbes which cause acne lesions. Furthermore, its drying actions help shrink swollen acne lesions, leading to their rapid dissolution.

Treatment Protocol

Add a few drops of oil of oregano to liquid soaps or cleansers. Wash the face or affected region twice daily. After cleaning apply oil of oregano directly on the pimples in the morning and at night before bedtime. Simply dab a small amount of the oil directly upon the center of the acne lesion once or twice daily. Don't rub the oil vigorously into the skin. Just dab it on where needed. Also, take 2 to 5 drops of the oil under the tongue or in juice/water twice daily. For best results take Oregamax internally, 2 to 4 capsules twice daily. Adolescents may rebel at the taste of oil of oregano. Take wild oregano gelcaps, that is Oreganol, one capsule twice daily. However, the ideal method is to take it under the tongue.

With regular use improvement should be noted within a week. If rash or irritation occurs, discontinue use.

Animal bites

Animal bites cause a significant degree of pain, disability, and infection in America every year. Dog bites are by far the most common type. As many as two million Americans are bitten by dogs every year. While other animals, such as cats and wildlife, also bite, their bites are insignificant numerically compared to dog bites. The postal service is aware of the danger of dog bites, as thousands of mail carriers are bitten by dogs every year. Dog bites are an enormous cause of disability. Regarding the role of cats and other animals it is interesting to note that human bites are the second most common type of "animal" bite.

Any animal bite can readily become infected. This is because bites are a type of puncture wound wherein contaminated secretions are deeply lodged. Deep puncture wounds are at a high risk of becoming infected, much more so than superficial wounds. One reason is that the microbes are essentially seeded directly into the blood and tissues, because of the depth of the wound. In puncture wounds less oxygen is available, because the circulation is poorer in the muscles and other deep tissues than in the more superficial layers of the skin. Oxygen impedes the growth of microbes, and it is the circulation which is responsible for delivering the body's anti-infection team: the white blood cells. This reduced blood, nutrient, and oxygen flow contributes to the high risk for potentially life threatening infections.

Dog bites notoriously become infected, in fact, the rule is that any dog bite which breaks the skin will become infected. This is why physicians often fail to suture severe dog bite wounds. The closing of the wound only serves to hold the infection within the tissues. The result is poor wound healing as well as potentially life threatening infections. There are those who suggest that dog saliva is "clean" or "less noxious than human saliva." However, this is far from the case: dogs are carnivores, and their saliva teems with microbes.

Oil of oregano is a life saving medicine for animal bite victims. It penetrates the deepest recesses of puncture wounds, killing pathogens on contact. No other antiseptic can match its capacity to cure puncture wound infections. Furthermore, it reduces inflammation and halts pain in bite wounds, while neutralizing the toxicity of injected venom or secretions. As a result of its dependable antiseptic powers oil of oregano saves limbs and lives.

Treatment protocol

Wash the wound thoroughly and seek medical attention, if necessary. Thoroughly saturate the puncture site or open wound with the oil. Repeat application several times daily. For severe wounds use the SuperStrength oil of wild oregano, using as much as is necessary to saturate the wound region. As a side effect oil of oregano helps halt bleeding. Take a few drops of oil of oregano in water or juice two or three times daily. Also, take Oregamax, three capsules twice daily. To speed the healing of the wound and prevent scar formation take the following nutrients:

pantothenic acid	500 mg twice daily
folic acid	5 mg twice daily
vitamin C	500 mg twice daily
vitamin E	400 I.U. twice daily
vitamin A	25,000 I.U. once daily
selenium	200 mcg twice daily
zinc	25 mg twice daily

Arthritis

Arthritis is defined as inflammation of the joints. It may be caused by poor diet and is often aggravated by toxic reactions to specific foods. Infection is another major cause, and prolonged stress may also lead to arthritis.

Nutritional deficiency plays a major role in arthritis. The proper health of the joints is highly dependent upon a steady supply of nourishment in the form of amino acids, minerals, mucopolysaccharides, vitamins, and essential fatty acids. Arthritics are commonly deficient in a wide range of nutrients, including vitamin C, vitamin E, pantothenic acid, niacin, vitamin A, vitamin D, vitamin K, essential fatty acids, and mucopolysaccharides. Regarding the latter, popular treatments for arthritis include shark cartilage, chondroitin sulfate, and glucosamine sulfate, all of which are rich sources of mucopolysaccharides.

There are several types of arthritis and each has different causes. Infection by various germs, particularly parasites and bacteria, is the most common cause. Regardless of the cause the common thread is that the joints become terribly inflamed. That is why the primary medical treatment for arthritis consists of anti-inflammatory drugs.

Oil of oregano is a potent anti-inflammatory agent and exerts these effects both topically and internally. Plus, it is an anti-pain agent. A study published in *Phytotherapie Research* determined that oil of wild oregano exhibits morphine-like properties. The crushed herb, in the form of Oregamax, also exhibits anti-inflammatory powers. Furthermore, oregano products are far safer than the arthritis drugs such as aspirin, Motrin, and Indocin. The latter are the number one cause of intestinal bleeding and bleeding ulcers and, thus, are the major cause of sudden death in arthritics. Yet, perhaps the greatest function of the oil in the treatment of arthritis relates to its antiseptic action: oil of oregano destroys both parasites and bacteria.

Treatment Protocol

Rub oil of oregano on affected joints in the morning and before bedtime daily until the condition is resolved. For tougher situations use the SuperStrength oil of wild oregano. Take also Oregamax, three capsules twice daily.

Asthma

The incidence of asthma in the United States has reached virtual epidemic proportions and is rising exponentially every year. Perhaps the most disconcerting statistic is the fact that the death rate is also rising despite intensive medical treatment. Asthma deaths have risen some 300% in the past 20 years. While medical doctors claim the cause to be "mysterious," the fact is evidence exists that asthma medicines increase the risk of death from asthma attacks and that asthmatics not taking drugs live longer than medically treated individuals. Obviously, medical treatment has entirely failed regarding this disease.

The modern diet is directly related to the genesis of asthma. The fact is this disease is rare in societies subsisting on a native diet. Processed foods contain a wide range of chemicals, many of which provoke asthma attacks. The primary culprits include food dyes, sulfites, MSG, nitrates, artificial colors, and processed vegetable oils. For individuals with asthma processed foods are taboo. In order to minimize the risk a natural food diet free of additives must be constructed. However, certain foods, even though entirely natural, may provoke asthma attacks. This occurs through the phenomenon known as food allergy. Common culprits include citrus fruit, peanuts, wheat, seafood, and milk products. There is one word of caution: oregano is a spice, and allergy to spices is relatively common. Although the potential for allergic reactions to a wild spice is quite low, still, individuals sensitive to the mint family may also have an allergic reaction to oregano. However, the majority of allergic reactions to oregano are an intolerance to the commercially available spices, which are entirely different botanically from the medicinal herb. The fact is wild oregano has been used historically to relieve constricted breathing. It possesses both anti-mucus and anti-cough properties. However, if breathing worsens when taking oregano, discontinue use immediately. For further information regarding the role of food allergy in asthma see *How to Eat Right and Live Longer (formerly Eat Right to Live Long)*, by Dr. Cass Ingram, Knowledge House Publishers.

Infection is another major factor in the cause of asthma. Often, asthma is provoked by a combined effect of poor diet plus infection. Sites of infection include the lungs, bronchial tubes, sinuses, and even the teeth.

It has been long known that acute infections, such as colds, flu, croup, sore throat, or pneumonia, may instigate asthma attacks. However, what is less well known is the fact that chronic infection, particularly infections by fungi and yeasts, may be a primary cause of asthma. What this implies is that hidden infections within the body may induce the disease itself and that the eradication of the infection is necessary before the asthma can be cured. Likely sites of infection include the lungs, kidneys, liver, spleen, bowel, sinuses, and roots of the teeth. Remember, the incidence of asthma and the degree of its complications have gotten worse, not better. Something else besides constant consumption of bronchodilators, cortisone, and theophylline must be done. Oil of oregano is one of those answers aiding in the eradication of this dreaded disease. Certainly, the ancients knew of its value for this disorder and prescribed it routinely.

Treatment protocol

In the event of an asthma attack rub oil of oregano on the chest. Repeat several times daily. Also, directly inhale vapors from the bottle. Take a few drops under the tongue or in juice/water two or three times daily. During an acute attack take oreganol gelcaps, 1 or 2 capsules every few hours. Use Oregamax on a daily basis as a preventive, three capsules twice daily.

Athlete's foot

Athlete's foot is perhaps the most common fungal infection of humans, afflicting untold millions of individuals. It is caused by a fungus known as a dermatophyte, and this is defined as an organism that survives on skin, specifically the layers of dead skin that are continuously shed by the body. The dermatophytes essentially make a meal of the proteins and sugars found in skin and have a particular affinity for the protein known as keratin from which skin, hair, and nails are made. Infections by dermatophytes are known more commonly as ringworm.

Dermatophytes invade the skin usually through injured or diseased regions. However, they are capable of directly invading human tissue, because they secrete powerful protein digesting enzymes, and this is how infection spreads. Once skin infection becomes established, the organisms are difficult to destroy. The immune system of its own accord nearly always fails to eradicate existing dermatophyte infestations. This is partly because of the location of the infection and is also the result of the fungal defense plan. Dermatophytes secrete chemicals into the body which block the immune system's ability to destroy them. For the fungus it is a matter of self preservation.

Once the fungus gains a foothold, it is difficult to eradicate. The organism invades no deeper than the various layers of the skin as well as the deep recesses of the nail bed. There, it feeds directly upon the dead skin cells, plus it produces toxins and enzymes which destroy cells so it can use them as food. Furthermore, the organism thrives upon sugar, which is delivered to it through the blood in the form of glucose. High sugar consumption significantly increases the growth rate of althlete's foot fungus.

When the fungus grows, it produces toxins, which are responsible for itching and irritation. At times the itching is so extreme that the individual excoriates himself/herself. When this happens, the raw wound may become secondarily infected by bacteria. This may be manifested by inflammation, swelling, and foul odor.

As the name implies athlete's foot is usually the result of direct contact of the feet with the fungus in public settings such as gymnasiums and showers. However, it may also be contracted in the "private sector," again by contact with moist surfaces such as the floors, shower tiles, or tubs in hotels or homes, where the organism thrives. The fungus is disseminated from these regions onto the skin of an unsuspecting individual, where it may readily thrive. If the feet are not carefully cleaned and dried or if there is a cut on the foot, it may aggressively invade the tissues. This fungus has a particular propensity for attacking the webbing between the fourth and fifth toes, and this is where infection usually begins. Circulation is poorest in the foot in this region, which means that there is less oxygen and nutrients being delivered. Dermatophytes prefer tissue with low oxygen content, since oxygen is a fungal poison.

Oil of oregano outright destroys this disgusting fungus. The organism is defenseless against the oil's potent chemistry, since oregano oil contains solvents capable of disabling the fungal cell membrane. Researchers document how oil of oregano destroys all traces of dermatophytes in the test tube, and this is equally the case for human infections. However, it is important to realize that infections by dermatophytes are usually chronic, meaning the organism is well established within the host. The fact is if the infection is prolonged, the organism infects the tissues deep enough to evade the immune defenses. Because of the chronicity, it may take a relatively long period of treatment before the infection is eradicated. As long as improvement is noted keep using the oil. Even if it takes weeks or months before a resolution is noted, it is well worth the effort.

Treatment protocol

Apply oil of oregano liberally to the affected regions of the feet, being sure to also treat regions between the toes. Repeat this application two or three times daily until the infection is cured. Always apply the oil to the feet after contact with public surfaces such as the floors of school showers, athletic clubs, and bathtubs/floors in hotels, etc.

For toenail fungus apply the oil directly to the nail and nail bed in large amounts. Also, gently rub it between the toes. Take several drops of the oil in juice, milk, or water twice daily or fill a small gelatin capsule with the oil and take one or two daily with meals. Remember, toenail fungus is a chronic and difficult-to-treat condition. Do not expect results overnight. For best results also take the oil internally, like 2 to 5 drops under the tongue twice daily.

Bad Breath

Bad breath usually has one primary cause: microbial overgrowth in the mouth. However, it may also develop as a result of an imbalance in the intestinal tract, and foul odors can be transmitted from the gut to the mouth. In fact, constipated individuals frequently have bad breath. This is particularly true for those who have had no bowel movement for several days. It is abnormal to have only one bowel movement per day let alone one per week or month. Wastes which fester in the body may produce foul odor which will emanate through the breath or elsewhere.

Bad breath, known medically as halitosis, has no cure in modern medicine. However, virtually everyone is familiar with the marketing efforts of mouthwash companies, proclaiming their products "fight bad breath" by killing microbes. The majority of these mouthwashes contain alcohol as the active ingredient, which may be found in concentrations as high as 30%. This means there is a greater amount of alcohol in some mouthwashes than there is in wine. Recent studies document how the alcohol in mouthwashes induces damage to the oral mucosa and significantly increases the risk for a variety of cancers, including esophageal, neck, and oral cancer. Yet, the main issue is that mouthwashes are impotent in antimicrobial powers compared to oil of oregano. This oil destroys a wide range of oral pathogens, and, thus, it is highly effective in eradicating bad breath. A study by Weber State University determined that oil of oregano readily destroys oral pathogens. Carcinogenicity is not a concern with oil of oregano, rather, by destroying potentially invasive microbes it aids in the prevention of oral, esophageal, and neck cancers.

Treatment protocol

Rub a few drops of oil of oregano on the gums and teeth morning and night. Use the oil on a toothbrush instead of toothpaste. Usually, foul odor in the mouth should become diminished immediately. Regular use will ultimately create a fresh sensation in the mouth, and bad breath will be eliminated. Furthermore, the regular use of this oil will lead to a reduction in plaque formation.

Bed Sores and Ulcerations

Bed sores occur in the elderly and infirm. However, ulcerations of the skin may afflict individuals with diabetes and poor circulation. Varicose ulcers, also known as stasis ulcers, occur as a result of impaired circulation in the veins. Individuals with a history of severe varicose veins are highly vulnerable to the development of these ulcers.

Any open wound of the skin can readily become infected, especially in individuals with compromised immunity. If untreated, such infections may spread into the blood, causing blood poisoning, i.e. sepsis. If applied directly upon an open wound as soon as it develops, oil of oregano will prevent such potentially disastrous infections.

Diabetics are at a high risk for the development of open wounds, and these are appropriately known as diabetic ulcers. The wounds develop primarily upon the extremities, especially the lower legs and feet. The vulnerability is due to the fact that diabetics suffer from compromised circulation, lowered immunity, and delayed wound healing. The point is that with diabetics even a minor injury can lead to ulcer development. Since they lack the protective mechanisms for normal wound healing, a potential disaster is brewing. Usually, once the wound fails to heal and an ulcer forms, it readily becomes infected.

In a hospital setting infected bed sores and open wounds are often impossible to rapidly cure. Surgery and/or antibiotics usually aggravate the problem. The infected ulcers may continue to grow in size and may cause extreme pain and tissue damage. In diabetics the healing is poor, and infection readily spreads. Ultimately, this may result in gangrene and, thus, amputation. Oil of oregano can save limbs and lives. It will eradicate virtually any type of infection occurring in bed sores or for that matter any type of open wound. If used aggressively in hospitals, it would greatly aid in the prevention of wound infection as well as in stimulating the prompt healing of wounds. Furthermore, it would undoubtedly significantly reduce the occurrence of gangrene resulting from diabetic ulcers.

Treatment protocol

Saturate the open wound with oil of oregano; cover, if necessary. Repeat dressing every twelve hours. To speed healing and strengthen immunity take Oregamax, three capsules three times daily until the wound heals.

Bladder infections

There seems to be no medical cure for bladder infections. While antibiotics may halt an initial infection, often the condition develops chronically, and antibiotics become ineffective. Furthermore, the prolonged use of antibiotics leads to infection of the bladder by drug-resistant microbes, particularly E. coli and Candida albicans.

Physicians know that antibiotics are overused for this condition. They simply don't know there are other options. Because of the massive use of antibiotics, a variety of antibiotic-resistant bacterial infections develop within the bladder and urinary tract, and these infections are difficult to eradicate. Common culprits include E. coli, Proteus, Klebsiella, staph, and strep. However, fungal infection of the urinary tract is perhaps the most common microbial consequence of antibiotic overuse. Here, the fungus readily colonizes the bladder, urethra, vagina, and even the kidneys. Symptoms of urinary fungal infection can be devastating and may include constant bladder pressure, frequent urination, night urination, dribbling, bladder pressure/pain, low back pain, flank pain, burning or pain upon urination, urgency, and incontinence.

Because these mutant microbes are notoriously difficult to destroy with standard antibiotic therapy, natural antiseptics must be utilized as adjunctive treatment. Such substances include garlic, onion, goldenseal, echinacea, balsam, chlorophyll, cloves, and oregano.

Oil of oregano offers significant antiseptic powers for the urinary tract. It is far more active against obnoxious urinary pathogens than the typically relied upon natural compounds such as garlic, goldenseal, and echinacea. The active ingredient, carvacrol, acts directly upon the mucus membranes of the urinary tract and bladder, aiding in the destruction of noxious microbes. It offers the unique advantage of destroying both urinary bacteria as well as yeasts, something that standard antibiotics fail to achieve.

Treatment protocol

Apply the oil directly over the bladder region, i.e. the region between the belly button and pubic symphysis. For women mix a few drops of the oil in a tablespoon of coconut fat or cocoa butter. Immerse in the vaginal tract; be prepared for heat sensation. Vaginal application allows for indirect absorption into the blood, plus the vagina and bladder are adjacent anatomically. Take a few drops of oil of oregano under the tongue twice daily. Or, fill a small gelatin capsule and take one twice daily with meals; or, simply take the Oreganol gelcaps, one or two capsules twice daily. Also, take the Oregamax, three capsules three times daily.

Bromidrosis

This is the medical term for the foul odor that is associated with excessive or constant sweating of the skin. It occurs particularly in the feet, groin, and axilla. The excessive sweating is caused by weakness of the adrenal glands and/or overactivity of the autonomic nervous system. The sweating is a problem not only because it is uncomfortable but also because the excess moisture encourages bacterial and fungal growth, which results in the production of a foul odor.

Oil of oregano is a natural deodorant. It helps reduce excessive sweat gland production, while destroying the microbes which cause body odor. It effectively eliminates the odor of bromidrosis, and improvement is often noted immediately.

Treatment protocol

Simply apply the oil to the axilla, groin, or on the soles of the feet and between the toes twice daily. For women, do not apply to the axilla immediately after shaving, as this may result in a burning sensation. This treatment usually halts the odor quickly and in many cases will reduce or eliminate the sweating.

Boils

Boils are a type of infection of the skin, usually involving the skin ducts surrounding the hair follicles or the sebaceous glands. There are two types of boils: furuncles and carbuncles. Furuncles are infections of the hair ducts, that is the root from which the hairs arise. Carbuncles are infections of the sebaceous glands; they are generally more extensive and are of a potentially more serious nature than furuncles.

Boils are usually caused by bacterial infection, although infections by fungi, particularly Candida albicans, may also be involved. Staph is the most common culprit, and strep may also be involved. All of these microbes are aggressive and toxic pathogens.

It was once thought that normal flora, that is the bacteria which are normal inhabitants of the skin and those which line the various skin ducts, are a factor in the cause of acne. However, recent research proves that these delicate or "healthy" bacteria are not the cause of disease. Rather, these bacteria protect the glands, ducts, and skin from becoming infected by noxious microbes. In fact, certain of these bacteria produce natural antibiotics, which block the growth of the pathogens. Rather, it is when the balance of these natural bacteria is disrupted, such as might result from prolonged antibiotic therapy, that skin infections typically develop. Interestingly, one researcher and author of a book on antibiotics noted that he developed a severe case of boils, which erupted all over his back, after a course of tetracycline. The point is that once the good bacteria of the skin are decimated the field is open for invasion by noxious and destructive microbes.

Nutritional deficiency plays a role in the genesis of boils. A lack of essential fatty acids, vitamin B-2, vitamin B-6, folic acid, and zinc increases the likelihood of boil formation. Essential fatty acids act as natural antibiotics, plus they help maintain the normal secretory activity of the sebaceous glands. Zinc and B-6 are required for the proper metabolism of essential fatty acids, and all of these nutrients are needed to keep the sebaceous glands in optimal health. Vitamin B-2, or riboflavin, is needed for cell oxygenation. Normal skin cell and sebaceous cell growth is dependent upon folic acid as well as zinc.

Boils are often painful as well as unsightly. Furthermore, if left untreated, infection may spread throughout the body. Recurrent boils occurring in various regions of the body are a signal of chronic internal infection, usually from staph or strep. The point is that the infection is being seeded to the skin from inside the body.

Medical treatment for boils is generally futile. Excision and drainage may provide relief, but the boils usually recur. Antibiotics usually fail to eradicate them and standard antiseptics are largely impotent. In fact, excessive use of antibiotics encourages the growth of the microbes which cause boils.

Oil of oregano is highly effective against boils. Applied topically, it aggressively penetrates the boils, delivering its potent action deep into the hair follicles and sebaceous ducts. Furthermore, because of its solvent action, the oil helps dehydrate boils, which aids in the destruction of the microbes. Microbes, which are over 90% water, have difficulty surviving in a dry environment. For optimal results take the oil internally as well as topically.

Treatment protocol

Apply oil of oregano directly on the boil(s) twice daily. Take two or more drops under the tongue once daily. Also, take Oregamax, three capsules twice daily.

Bronchitis

The medical profession insists that the cause of bronchitis is unknown. The attitude is that there is no cure. What is certain is that the standard medical approach to bronchitis, that is the administration of potent antibacterial agents, is erroneous. This is because this condition is caused by a totally different organism: molds. The molds are inhaled on dust or directly from mold-infested areas. They become deposited in the moist and nutrient-rich bronchial tubules. There they find a fertile growth medium to multiply in the billions. The molds produce toxins, which irritate the lungs and bronchi, causing mucus production, difficulty breathing, and cough. The fact is the mold/fungus infection is the most common cause of a chronic irritating cough from non-bacterial causes.

Antibiotics have failed to reverse this condition, because these drugs kill only bacteria, which are only a minor cause. Unless the molds and fungi are killed the condition persists.

Oil of wild oregano is a potent agent for reversing mold infestation. Its aggressive natural chemicals are toxic to molds. A study performed by Turkish investigators proved that even the most dangerous molds, like aspergillus, were neutralized by the oil.

Treatment protocol

Take Oreganol™ oil of wild oregano under the tongue, 5 or more drops twice daily. Take also Oregamax crushed wild oregano capsules, 3 or more capsules twice a day. Inhale the oil and vaporize it around the home. In a spray bottle simply add a few drops to 6 ounces of hot water; spray about the home, especially in areas contaminated by mold.

Bruises

Bruises are caused as a result of ruptured blood vessels. When the blood vessels burst, the contents spill into the tissues resulting in discoloration. This may be due to trauma, but individuals who bruise easily know that bruises may appear seemingly without cause. This is a consequence of a weakening of the blood vessel walls. If the walls are strong, mild trauma or pressure cannot result in a bruise. However, if the blood vessel walls are friable, seemingly insignificant events, such as leaning against a counter or desk or the firm grasp of a hand, might cause a bruise.

Easy bruising is a warning of nutritional deficiency. The blood vessel walls require a steady supply of a variety of nutrients to maintain patency and integrity. For further information regarding the role of nutrients in preventing bruising, blood blisters, etc., see the *Self-Test Nutrition Guide* or the highly sophisticated web site for determining nutritional deficiencies, NutritionTest.com.

Oil of oregano is a solvent, so it helps dissipate bruises. Its ability in this regard is both remarkable and quick. Furthermore, its anti-inflammatory powers aid in reducing the pain and swelling associated with large or traumatic bruises.

Treatment protocol

Apply oil of oregano directly upon bruised tissue. Repeat two or three times daily. In the event of trauma, to prevent or minimize bruising apply oil of oregano immediately to the involved site(s).

Burns

The old homeopathic adage of "treating like with like" certainly applies to the use of oil of oregano with burns. When applied topically, this oil induces a hot sensation, and yet, it is highly effective when applied directly upon burns. In fact, in an action similar to homeopathics, the heat from the oregano somehow cures the burned tissue.

Oil of oregano's potent anti-inflammatory powers are readily evident by the fact that it immediately halts the swelling/pain which typically occurs in burns. Although there may be discomfort initially dramatic improvement in the pain and swelling will result from its application. Furthermore, the oil helps halt blistering. Perhaps of greatest importance is the fact that sterility will be created within the burn. This is critical, because infection is the major cause of post-burn complications, and this is especially true of third degree burns, the type that requires hospitalization. If it were used in hospital burn wards oil of wild oregano would save thousands of lives each year by preventing infection. Plus, it would save individuals from untold pain and the brutality of disfigurement, since the oil prevents, indeed reverses, scar formation.

Treatment protocol

Oil of oregano is the ideal burn cure. It works fast and reliably. Simply apply oil of oregano to the burn as soon as possible after injury. Repeat application two or three times daily or as often as is needed to curb pain. For tougher situations use the SuperStrength variety. Also, take oil of oregano under the tongue, 2 or more drops twice daily. If the burn is severe and fails to heal rapidly, see your physician immediately.

Bursitis

This is an inflammation of the lining of the joint, the latter being known as the bursa. The bursa is a sac containing synovial fluid, which lines and cushions the joints. When this joint lining becomes inflamed, pain and swelling of the joint results.

Bursitis may result from trauma, but it also may result from overuse of the joint such as might occur from sports and manual labor. It may also be caused by nutritional deficiency. In the 1950s it was discovered that bursitis of the shoulders was associated with calcium deposits in the bursal sacs. Interestingly, researchers reasoned that the calcium deposits were the result of B-12 deficiency. When the vitamin was administered via injections, the calcium deposits disappeared, and the bursitis was cured.

Frozen shoulder syndrome is, in essence, an extreme type of bursitis. In this condition the inflammation within the bursae (pl. of bursa) and within the shoulder tissues becomes so extensive that the shoulder joint becomes immobilized, i.e. frozen. Severe inflammation leads to a thickening of the lubricating compounds of the joint linings. In a sense, these compounds become "sticky." The muscles and connective tissues seize against the bones of the shoulder joint like the rods or pistons of a motor might seize if there is a lack of lubrication.

Oil of oregano is a solvent, and thus, it helps normalize thickened tissue secretions, including synovial fluid. Its anti-inflammatory properties and its tremendous penetrating power make it an ideal rub in the event of bursitis and/or frozen shoulder syndrome. If using North American Herb and Spice's Oil of Oregano, the purest grade of extra virgin olive oil is added. The olive oil itself is a lubricant, aiding in relaxing tight muscles and the softening of tense or thickened tissues.

Treatment protocol

Rub oil of oregano over the involved joint several times daily. Repeat as necessary. Take a few drops in juice, water, or milk once or twice daily.

Candidiasis

This fungal infection is a major cause of illness in America today. Millions of Americans suffer from some form of Candida albicans infection, the latter being one of the few types of yeasts capable of invading human tissue. The organism may infect virtually any part of the body, although the most commonly involved sites include the nail beds, skin folds, feet, mouth, sinuses, ear canal, umbilicus, esophagus, intestines, vaginal tract, and urethra. Once the organism gains a foothold, it is difficult to eradicate, and this is especially true of Candida infections of the skin, nails, and mucous membranes. Candida may also infect the internal organs, and this results in serious disease. Likely sites of infection include the thyroid gland, adrenal glands, kidneys, bladder, bowel, esophagus, uterus, lungs, and bone marrow.

Candida albicans infection has historically been regarded as a women's problem, as in, for instance, the yeast infection of vaginitis. However, recently it has been determined that men and women are essentially equally likely to develop the infection. In fact men are more likely than women to suffer from internal fungus infection, largely because they fail to seek treatment. Major sites of infection in men include the skin, prostate, urethra, kidneys, fingernails, intestines, esophagus, and bladder.

A number of factors increase the likelihood of fungal infection. These include antibiotic therapy, high sugar diet, antacids, cortisone, chemotherapy, radiation, birth control pills, chronic alcohol consumption, drug abuse, sexual promiscuity, poor hygiene, and chewing tobacco. In women excessive douching may precipitate vaginal candidiasis. Bubble bath solutions are also a culprit, since they contain chemicals which damage the delicate vaginal membranes and alter vaginal pH. Yeasts tend to grow in alkaline pH, and the normal vaginal pH is acidic. Commercial soaps of all kinds, particularly bubble bath solutions, are lye based, meaning they are alkaline. The so-called dishpan hand syndrome of home-keepers is likely a Candida infection. Constant immersion of the hands in water potentiates yeast growth, because yeasts thrive on moist surfaces. Furthermore, soap damages the protective oily lining of the skin, increasing the risk for fungal infection.

Treatment protocol

If the infection is topical, apply oil of oregano as needed several times daily. For internal infections take five or more drops under the tongue two or three times daily. Follow this regimen for two to three weeks, then take two drops twice daily under the tongue as a maintenance. With Candida infections of the mucous membranes oregano can be used comfortably only in the mouth and within the gut. Application upon the genitals, vagina, or rectum is highly uncomfortable, leading to severe hot sensations. Thus, using it undiluted on sensitive regions is not advised. For application in these regions dilute a drop or two of oil of oregano into a tablespoon of olive oil or, preferably, coconut oil. Apply gently to the involved region; do not rub the solution aggressively on sensitive regions, such as the genitals, as this may lead to irritation and pain. Six to twelve capsules of Oregamax daily is also recommended for long term treatment of chronic or stubborn infections. Also, for tougher situations take wild oregano oil gelcaps, one or two capsules twice daily.

Canker sores

This is one of the most painful of all types of lesions. Canker sores occur on the mucous membranes, primarily in the mouth. They are painful, inflamed, and often infected ulcerations that are generally difficult to treat. Another problem is that they tend to heal slowly.

Canker sores are a warning sign of disrupted immunity. They often develop as a result of toxic reactions to foods. The foods poison the immune system. The immune cells over-react and produce a variety of harsh compounds. The compounds are toxic to the mucous membranes and canker sores develop in the melee. Foods which commonly provoke canker sores include chocolate, strawberries, raspberries, wheat, rye, malt, nuts, milk products, butter, processed meats, fried foods, tomatoes, and citrus.

Many theories have been advanced regarding the infectious causes of canker sores. While viruses may be involved the most likely culprit is a bacterium: group A strep. This type of strep is capable of producing enzymes, which can destroy, that is ulcerate, mucous membranes. Researchers in Utah recently proved that oil of oregano thoroughly destroys oral strep.

Treatment protocol

Apply oil of oregano directly to the canker sores. Saturate pieces of cotton and deposit over the wound. Take crushed wild oregano capsules (e.g. Oregamax), two capsules twice daily.

Cellulitis

This is defined as large scale inflammation and infection of the layers of skin cells. To explain this further, a boil or acne is skin infection, but it is localized. With cellulitis, the infection and inflammation spread in an uncontrolled fashion.

Cellulitis occurs when microbes overwhelm the structural and immunological defenses within the skin tissues. Normally, surface infections are readily walled off within the skin tissues to prevent dissemination. Obviously, cellulitis is a potentially serious illness, because blood poisoning may occur.

Erysipelas is a variant of cellulitis usually affecting the skin and subcutaneous tissues of the face and neck. It is evidenced by extreme inflammation, pain, hot sensation, and bright redness of the skin (the prefix ery is derived from the Greek erythros, meaning red) accompanied by fever, chills, nausea, and vomiting. This type of infection is more common in adults than impetigo, in fact, the primary victims are the elderly. It is caused by strep infection.

Treatment protocol

Apply oil of oregano over the involved region by dabbing gently with a saturated cotton ball. Discard after use. Repeat at least once daily. Take a few drops of oil of oregano twice daily in milk, juice, or water. Also, take Oregamax, three capsules three times daily.

Cold Sores

These painful and annoying lesions are caused by a virus and are actually a type of herpes infection. The type of herpes involved is the same as the one which causes chicken pox. After causing chicken pox the virus lives dormant in the body, residing within the deep recesses of the nervous system, specifically regions in the nerves known as ganglia. Here it is held at bay by the immune system.

Cold sores, that is oro-facial herpetic infections, arise as the result of some sort of toxic insult, whether it be stress, infectious illness (colds, flu, sore throat, pneumonia, etc), food allergy, alcohol abuse, drug abuse, too much sunlight, cold exposure, or toxic chemical exposure. Furthermore, a number of pharmaceutical drugs may precipitate an attack of cold sores, particularly aspirin, Motrin, Indocin, Clinoril, Cardiazem (or other calcium channel blockers), Procardia, and cortisone. In particular, cortisone greatly increases the invasive powers of herpes viruses.

Oil of oregano is one of the few substances proven to kill herpes viruses. A study done by Sidiqqui determined that the oil completely destroyed herpes viruses, "disintegrating" them.

Treatment protocol

Apply oil of oregano directly to the cold sore as soon as possible, that is when you feel it beginning to erupt. The sooner it is applied the greater will be the positive effects. In fact, if it is applied soon enough, it may stop the formation altogether. If not, keep applying the oil several times daily. Simply dab a small amount of oil onto the lesion. It takes the pain away immediately, keeps the cold sore from enlarging, and facilitates the healing. Do not rub it vigorously into the lesion, as this may lead to pain and irritation. When the oil is applied to the lips a burning sensation is normal, so be gentle. Take a drop or two of oil of oregano twice daily under the tongue. Consume Oregamax, three capsules twice daily.

Colds/flu

Wouldn't it be nice to make it through a year without getting a cold or flu? While usually not life threatening, they can cause a great deal of misery. This is unnecessary, because colds and flu are largely preventable. In fact, the flu can be a serious illness, and over 50,000 Americans, mostly the elderly, die every year as a result of it.

It isn't necessary to get the flu this year, and you could avoid colds as well by using oil of oregano as a dependable antiviral remedy. Both the oil and the crushed herb exhibit antiviral powers, in other words, they can kill viruses directly. Furthermore, they enhance the body's antiviral defenses by boosting white blood cell function and increasing lymph flow.

Oil of oregano has been utilized since ancient times as a cure for the common cold. It is active against the cold virus as well as the various burdensome symptoms associated with colds. Stubborn cold symptoms, such as runny nose, congestion, chills, sore throat, earaches, cough, post nasal drip, muscle aches, fever, fatigue, and stuffy sinuses, all may be relieved through its application. The fact is oil of wild oregano is a cure for the common cold.

Oil of oregano is also invaluable for the flu, both for prevention and cure. It is certainly superior to the flu shot. What is little known is the fact that flu shots have side effects. Some of these side effects are life-threatening.

Case History: a dear friend of mine had a flu shot. Within a few months he developed a severe heart disorder manifested by shortness of breath, exhaustion, and chest pain, leading to a heart attack. Prior to this he was completely free of heart disease and had no family history of it. Doctors informed him that he was one of hundreds of people who appear to have developed a bizarre heart disorder: heart muscle degeneration syndrome, in other words, his heart was being eaten away. The culprit, according to his doctor, was the flu vaccine.

Treatment protocol

Take two drops of oil of oregano daily as preventive medicine along with three capsules daily of Oregamax. If a cold or flu strikes, triple this dosage until the symptoms are resolved. If it is a tough case take the oil and Oregamax capsules more frequently, like every hour. In addition, the oil may be inhaled to relieve head cold symptoms.

Cough

A cough is a symptom rather than a disease. Usually, it is a symptom of lung disease or an acute infection of the respiratory passages. For instance, respiratory infections in children often begin as a mild cough. On a more serious note lung cancer often presents as an unrelenting cough, which is worse in the morning. However, millions of individuals suffer from chronic cough, and the cause is often never determined.

Regardless of the cause cough is an annoyance. Often, the cough is unrelenting and nothing seems to provide relief. Individuals suffering with chronic cough know well that the typical over-the-counter medicines, as well as prescription drugs, are largely impotent in ameliorating this condition.

The essential oils in oregano possess a medicinal effect called antitussive action. This means that they can halt a cough. This capacity of oregano has been known since ancient Egyptian times, and it has been used as a premier cure for lung disorders, including cough, for thousands of years. The oil is currently being evaluated in a clinical setting in the treatment of cough. Of the twenty individuals so far tested, all noted significant relief of cough after taking either the oil or the crushed herb. Many have reported an outright cure.

Treatment protocol

Inhale the oil of oregano directly from the bottle as often as possible. Take a few drops of the oil under the tongue twice daily or gargle with a few drops in salt water. For tougher situations use the SuperStrength oil of oregano, a few drops as needed. Also, take Oregamax capsules, 3 caps twice daily.

Cryptosporidium

This is a parasitic infection caused by a protozoan, a type of parasite which commonly contaminates soil and fresh water. The source of the infective organism is animal and human excrement.

The importance of cryptosporidium in causing human illness has only recently been appreciated and, in fact, previously it was thought to develop only rarely. In 1993 a massive outbreak occurred in Milwaukee. Fully 400,000 people, nearly one half the population, became infected as the result of ingesting contaminated water. Dozens of people died. Recently (1996), in Canada an entire lake was contaminated with the organism, and, despite public water treatment and chlorination, a boil order was in place for thousands of people for several months. Obviously, neither modern medicine nor sanitation offers any answers for this dangerous infection.

Cryptosporidium is difficult to kill, and there are no effective drugs available. When it invades the body, it tends to hide by burrowing into intestinal walls. Furthermore, it may invade cells in the liver and may do the same in red blood cells. It protects itself from destruction through converting into a cyst. However, the organism is no match for essential oil of oregano. Because of its solvent action oregano oil damages the cystic wall, leading to the destruction of the organism.

Treatment protocol

Take oil of oregano under the tongue, two drops twice daily. Consume a few drops twice daily in juice or milk. Take Oregamax, three capsules three times daily. Treatment must be aggressive and prolonged; this organism is rather difficult to kill. However, oil of oregano is active against it.

Dandruff and Seborrhea

Did you know that medical textbooks list dandruff, as well as seborrhea, as a type of disease? In other words, those flakes on the scalp are not entirely innocuous. Whether deemed dandruff or seborrhea, they are a sign of fungal infection. The glands and skin cells of the scalp are vulnerable to becoming infected by a variety of fungi. These fungi are responsible for the flaking and crusting, plus they are the main cause of itching of the scalp. Bacteria may infect the scalp, but this usually occurs as a result of trauma or is secondary to fungal infection. Both the scalp glands and the hair roots (i.e. follicles) are readily infected by fungi and bacteria.

Nutritional deficiency is another major factor causing scalp disorders. Tintera found that the infusion of several grams of vitamin B-6 intravenously via repeated doses eradicated dandruff/seborrhea. Other investigators note how scalp disorders are a warning of essential fatty acid deficiency and may also warn of biotin, riboflavin, and zinc deficiency. In my clinic a patient with severe seborrhea of the scalp was cured merely by taking large doses of essential fatty acids in the form of primrose oil. This makes sense, because not only do the essential fatty acids nourish the scalp, but they also act as natural antibiotics. However, the optimal treatment is to destroy the infection as well as resolve the deficiencies. For determining deficiencies in your body see the *Self-Test Nutrition Guide* (Dr. Cass Ingram, Knowledge House), a book designed for precise determination of an individual's nutritional needs. Or, use the nutritional deficiency web site, NutritionTest.com, a simple way to quickly determine your nutritional needs.

Treatment protocol

Add several drops of oil of oregano to shampoo and wash the hair and scalp thoroughly. Allow the shampoo to sit for two minutes before rinsing. Cover eyes and rinse. For added anti-dandruff effect rub a few drops into the scalp at night and wash off the next morning. Burning sensation may occur, but it is temporary. For internal antifungal treatment consume two drops of oil of oregano under the tongue twice daily. Take Oregamax, three capsules twice daily.

Diaper rash

Diaper rash is almost always due to fungal infection, and Candida albicans is the number one cause. Infants are highly vulnerable to the development of a variety of fungal infections, because their immune systems are underdeveloped, and, thus, they cannot mount a strong response against these organisms. Furthermore, if the mother has a vaginal yeast infection, the infant will assuredly develop one as a result of passage through the birth canal.

Careful hygiene is essential for the prevention of diaper rash. Moisture feeds fungus, and it is critical to frequently change diapers to prevent prolonged contact of the skin with urine or stool. Cloth diapers are advisable, as certain chemicals found in synthetic diapers damage local immunity and increase the risk for yeast infection. Be sure to rinse the genitals with water during each change. This significantly reduces the microbe count on the genital and buttocks regions. The hygiene of the caretaker is also important, and it is little appreciated that infections are readily transmitted from adult to infant. Be sure also to wash hands after each change; poor hand washing technique can lead to the transmission of infection to the baby as well as the rest of the family. Also, keep the fingernails clipped. A recent study documented how nurses spread infections to infants from dirty/long fingernails. One of the primary causes of outbreaks of infections within a family, such as Giardia, hepatitis, and dysentery, is negligence of proper hand washing, especially after contact with stool.

Treatment protocol

Dilute a drop or two of the oil in a tablespoon of olive oil. Apply to the involved region several times daily. If the rash persists or becomes aggravated, desist using the solution and see your physician.

Diarrhea

Diarrhea is a symptom rather than a disease. However, if it is unremitting, it can become pathological. Prolonged diarrhea leads to malabsorption of nutrients. Electrolyte depletion, that is the loss of sodium, potassium, chloride, and magnesium, is a serious consequence. If the depletion of these nutrients is extreme, physical collapse and even sudden death may occur.

Several illnesses may lead to diarrhea, and the most likely cause is intestinal infection. Parasites, viruses, and bacteria all may be the culprits. Other causes include food allergy and adrenal insufficiency. Regardless of the cause it is essential to halt the diarrhea as soon as possible.

Diarrhea may be the presenting symptom of food poisoning. In fact, this is the most common cause currently. The diarrhea of food poisoning is usually caused by bacterial infection, although parasitic infection, the major cause of diarrhea in third world countries, is becoming a primary cause in the United States. In fact, parasitic infection is now the number one cause of widespread outbreaks of diarrhea. A list of some of the predominant microbes responsible for diarrhea includes:

Salmonella	E. coli
Shigella	Enterobacter
Camphylobacter	flu virus
Clostridium	Candida albicans
Giardia	Cryptosporidium
Cyclospora	amoebas
tapeworms	hookworm
pinworm	roundworm
flukes cholera	

Oil of oregano is an ideal natural medicine for combating diarrhea, because it is active against a wide range of microbes. Researchers have shown that the oil destroys bacteria, fungi, viruses, and parasites, and very few compounds offer this broad spectrum of actions. One study found that septic water was sterilized by oil of oregano. The federal government proved that the oil quickly destroyed a wide range of germs which cause food poisoning, including the notorious drug resistant form of E. coli. This tremendous microbe-killing power makes oil of oregano unique as an antidiarrheal agent.

Treatment protocol

Take a few drops of oil of oregano two or three times daily in water or juice. For severe diarrhea fill a gelatin capsule with oil of oregano; take one capsule three times daily. Also, take Oregamax, three capsules three times daily. Avoid solid foods and consume instead broths, soups, and juices until the diarrhea abates. If the diarrhea is unrelenting, see your physician.

Ear infections

This is the greatest epidemic affecting American children. It is the main reason for childhood visits to doctors. Ironically, ear infections are entirely preventable.

The way ear infections are treated in medicine today, it is as if they are due to a deficiency of antibiotics. The fact that antibiotics are overused is no secret to the medical profession. According to Dr. James Hughes of the CDC (Centers for Disease Control) of the 110 million antibiotic prescriptions written yearly, one half are unnecessary. True, ears do become infected with bacteria and fungi, but usually the damage is precipitated by other causes, which are rarely if ever addressed. Allergic reactions to foods or perhaps viral respiratory infections are more likely the direct cause than bacterial infection. In other words, the bacterial infections are secondary to allergy and viruses. Here is how this works. When food allergy reactions occur, the mucous membranes of the sinuses become inflamed. This leads to blockage of a drainage duct known as the eustachian tube. When this tube becomes inflamed, it may collapse, leading to the accumulation of fluid/secretions in the middle ear. The secretions feed the growth of microbes, and potentially serious infections result. The same situation results from viral infections.

Deficiencies of a variety of nutrients may lead to ear infections. Children who develop repeated ear infections are usually severely deficient in vitamin A, vitamin C, riboflavin, pantothenic acid, folic acid, essential fatty acids, and selenium. Boosting the body levels of these nutrients increases the resistance against ear infections.

Usually, when a child is diagnosed with earaches or middle ear infections, nothing is done to resolve the nutritional deficiencies; certainly, few if any dietary alterations are made. Rather, repeated dosages of antibiotics are administered, which not only fail to cure the infections, but also actually increase the likelihood of future infections. An article in *Archives of Otolaryngology* describes how children who were aggressively treated with antibiotics at the beginning of ear infections were nearly 300% more likely to develop recurrent infections than those not treated at all. What's more, pediatric experts know that the placement of tubes does little or no good. Unfortunately, this procedure is largely motivated by financial reasons rather than any potential for cure.

Long term antibiotic usage in children leads to yet another problem: a variety of infections by antibiotic resistant microbes, particularly Candida albicans. It is virtually assured that any child who has undergone repeated treatment with antibiotics has a moderate to severe Candida infestation, and Candida can infect the ear, both inside and out. This may be manifested by a wide range of symptoms, including attention deficit, mood swings, depression, irritability, colic, constipation, rash, foul odor, uncontrollable sugar cravings, fatigue, bloating, sinus problems, and frequent infections.

Children are highly vulnerable to the toxic effects of antibiotics, and, because of their immature immune systems, they readily develop yeast infections. In children who have taken numerous prescriptions of antibiotics and who still have ear infections Candida infection of the ear should be suspected. Usually, if the ear is infected by the yeast, the rest of the body is also infected.

Treatment protocol

Oil of oregano is an outright cure for chronic earaches and is highly effective for acute ear infections as well. Simply take one or two drops in juice twice daily. Take Oregamax, two capsules three times daily. Apply the oil directly on the outer ear or near the outer ear. Do not put it into the ear. Nothing should be poured into the ear during an ear infection; do not drip the oil from a dropper directly into the ear. Be sure to place the oil on the outer ear by placing two or three drops on the finger and applying. Or, saturate a cotton ball and place it at the entrance of the ear canal.

Ebola and Dengue Fever

Both of these diseases are caused by a virus from the family known as arbovirus. They are also related in the fact that they are regarded as types of hemorrhagic fever. While currently rare in the United States there is a high likelihood that large scale infection could occur. However, a massive outbreak of dengue fever did occur in the southwestern United States in the 1920s, with some 700,000 people being infected in Texas alone. Unfortunately, dengue has recently resurfaced in this region, with cases being recorded in Texas, Arizona, and New Mexico. If the organism is uncontained, a major national disaster will result.

There is no medical treatment for either ebola or dengue, and perhaps this is what makes their invasion so disconcerting. However, if this occurs, oil of oregano can come to the rescue. One of the most potent naturally occurring antiviral agents known, oil of oregano would be an invaluable treatment for fighting these infections. The oil possesses a generalized antiviral action, plus it boosts immunity by accelerating the killing action of white blood cells and by improving lymph flow. In the event of infection by the ebola or dengue virus the oil should be used aggressively both internally and externally.

Treatment protocol

Rub the oil on any open wounds or sores. Dab on any suspect insect/mosquito bites. Take oil of oregano internally; take also Oreganol gelcaps, two capsules twice daily. Rub the oil liberally on any open wound or lesion. Take Oregamax, three capsules four times daily. In the event of a widespread outbreak of this life-destroying illness, use the oil liberally and take large doses of Oregamax, perhaps double the dosages mentioned.

Eczema

This is an inflammatory disease of the skin, which most commonly occurs in children. Regarded as an allergic disorder it is related to a general condition known as atopy. The latter is an inherited syndrome represented by a tendency to develop severe allergies, asthma, menstrual difficulty, and eczema. Researchers have discovered that atopy is related to disordered essential fatty acid metabolism as well as vitamin deficiency. Individuals with atopy and eczema are commonly deficient in essential fatty acids, riboflavin, pyridoxine, folic acid, magnesium, and zinc. The essential fatty acids are required for the development of healthy skin, and the body has a daily need for them. Interestingly, the proper metabolism of essential fatty acids within the skin is dependent upon ample supplies of riboflavin, pyridoxine, magnesium, and zinc, all of which are deficient in atopic individuals.

Eczema usually has an infective component. Rosenburg and colleagues from the University of Tennessee have discovered that eczematous lesions are actually infected chronically. The culprits include several varieties of fungi as well as staph and strep. What's more, the researchers discovered that when the organisms were killed, the eczema was cleared.

Unfortunately, physicians are largely unaware of the role of chronic infection in eczema. This is a travesty, because the wrong treatment is administered. Doctors give cortisone, both orally and topically, which is the exact opposite of what should be done. This is because cortisone depresses immunity and increases the risk of fungal and bacterial infection. True, cortisone creams often relieve symptoms and diminish eczematous lesions, but they fail to address the cause, and thus, no cure is achieved.

Oil of oregano is an ideal topical remedy for eczema. This is because it attacks the cause and also relieves symptoms. Oregano oil contains a variety of antiinflammatory compounds which reduce the swelling in eczematous lesions, halt itching, and stop scaling. The antiseptics in the oil effectively destroy microbes found within the lesions. The pure extra virgin olive oil soothes skin, and olive oil itself is an antifungal and antibacterial agent. Yet, its main value is via internal consumption, that is the destruction of the internal fungi which cause this condition.

Treatment protocol

Rub oil of oregano on all eczematous lesions twice daily. Take a few drops of the oil under the tongue twice daily. Also, mix a drop or two of the oil in juice, milk, or water and consume once or twice daily. Take Oregamax, three capsules twice daily. If irritation occurs, discontinue topical use and take it internally.

Fingernail fungus

This is yet another fungal epidemic striking the Western world. Tens of millions of Americans suffer from this disfiguring condition. No doubt, it is one of the major health problems of the modern world.

Fingernail fungus is caused primarily by the same organisms which cause ringworm and athlete's foot: the dermatophytes. The notorious Candida albicans is another common cause. Bacteria may be involved, but their role is secondary. The fungus invades the deep nail bed of the fingernail and takes up residence, feeding off the rich supply of keratin. It is difficult to eradicate with topical medicines, since the ability of the medicines to penetrate into the nail bed is poor.

A number of factors increase the likelihood for the development of fingernail fungus. These factors include a high sugar diet, skin or hand contact with noxious chemicals, the application of artificial nails, fingernail polish, alcohol abuse, and poor hygiene. Usually, it is thought that the infection arises from the outside environment, much like we might contract a cold or flu. In fact, the organism may arise from within the body and infect the nail bed through the bloodstream. What a horrible thought it is that fungus thrives within our bodies. Yet, the potential for being attacked is always there, since fungi, particularly yeasts, are commonly found in the body and live within us from birth to death.

Treatment protocol

Saturate the nail bed with oil of oregano. Ideally, soak the nails in hot water for a half hour. Then, apply the oil of oregano to the nail bed(s) in the oil. Leave the infected nail(s) in the soak for at least one half hour. Retain the soaking solution by covering and refrigerate for reuse. If rubbing on the nail bed, repeat twice daily. Take two drops of oil of oregano under the tongue twice daily. If the fungal nail infection is severe, fill a gelatin capsule with the oil and take one capsule daily with food. Continue treatment until condition is reversed.

Fleas

Fleas are becoming a virtual epidemic. In the year 2000 the entire baggage department of United Airlines became infested and airline attendants complained of having fleas. Fleas can be dangerous, as they may transmit a variety of microbial diseases, including the Plague. Usually, they are a mere irritant, however, they are always a cause of severe stress, both for animals and humans. Fleas are no contest for oil of oregano; it destroys them on contact.

Treatment protocol

Dab the oil of oregano on any suspect lesion. The fleas will be dead shortly. For severe infestation use the SuperStrength oil of oregano; add several drops to body soap and shampoo. Lather on the body and leave on as long as possible, then rinse. Repeat as needed. Also, dab the SuperStrength on the lesions as needed. Take the oil internaly, five or more drops twice daily.

Frostbite and frostburn

The occurrence of frostbite and/or frostburn is a medical emergency and, thus, requires immediate medical attention. Unfortunately, there is a paucity of medicines available in the emergency room for treating it, and certainly no advice is given on the topical administration of natural remedies. This is unfortunate, since there are a variety of natural substances which would prove useful in the event of this disastrous injury.

Oil of oregano is highly useful in frostbite/frostburn for a variety of reasons. It dramatically improves circulation to the skin and outer tissues; the increased blood flow minimizes tissue damage. It reduces inflammation as well as pain. It speeds healing, aiding in the regeneration of skin. Furthermore, it prevents infection from developing in open wounds.

Treatment protocol

Apply oil of oregano directly to the involved region. Repeat application as often as necessary; numerous applications may be necessary to achieve optimal response.

Giardiasis

Giardia infection, known medically as giardiasis, is caused by a parasite, the protozoan Giardia lamblia. Occurring throughout America this organism is found in the soil/water and is ubiquitous in the environment, as it is deposited through animal—and human—excrement. Large amounts of the organism are typically found in "natural" water sources such as mountain streams, ponds, lakes, and rivers. Just because water appears clean and is found in a remote place, this is no evidence of safety. In fact, a primary cause of Giardia outbreaks is drinking water from natural places such as fishing lakes and mountain streams.

Giardia infection can lead to significant disease and disability. Symptoms of infection include diarrhea, nausea, stomach pain, belching, foul gas, intestinal bloating, and weight loss. These symptoms are seen more commonly in children, who are, in fact, three times more likely to develop the infection than adults. Children with giardiasis often develop seemingly unrelated symptoms such as food allergy, irritability, attention deficit, uncontrollable behavior, headaches, and fatigue. In adults usually there are no symptoms, and, if they do exist, they are often mild such as stomach gas, intestinal gas, or bloating after eating. However, if left untreated, Giardia infection may lead to a variety of diseases, including psoriasis, eczema, arthritis, asthma, food allergy, hepatitis, fibromyalgia, chronic fatigue syndrome, attention deficit disorder, irritable bowel syndrome, Crohn's disease, ulcerative colitis, esophagitis, and bleeding ulcer. The connection between Giardia and these diseases is thought to be related to its invasive powers. The organism infects the lining of the digestive tract and also readily invades the liver. Damage to the intestinal wall can be extensive, leading to a condition known as leaky gut syndrome. Normally, the intestinal wall prevents the passage of large food particles or microbes into the blood; it is a protective barrier, preventing the blood and internal organs from exposure to poisons. However, if the gut wall is damaged, intestinal contents may "leak" into the blood. Giardia causes this by essentially boring holes into the intestinal membranes. Technically, this is known as increased intestinal permeability.

If infection of the gut is extensive, malabsorption of nutrients usually results. This is because when the parasites invade the intestinal lining, they damage the absorptive surface. The absorptive surface is made of millions of tiny finger-like projections known as intestinal villi. The villous projections look under a microscope like so many millions of tiny hair fibers. With giardiasis the villi are damaged and frequently are entirely flattened, in other words, the absorptive surface is lost. This leads to extensive nutritional deficiency, which further complicates the disease. This illustrates the critical importance of curing the infection. The organism must be destroyed so that the gut wall will heal.

Giardia is a stubborn organism and is both difficult to diagnose as well as kill. It has a propensity for invading the upper small intestine, where it bores deep into the intestinal wall. In this respect it is able to evade immune defenses. It may also be housed in the liver, where it invades the biliary tracts. Oil of oregano possesses deep penetrating powers and can readily penetrate the intestinal epithelium. In a study performed in Mexico, an area in which Giardia infection is endemic, oregano was more effective in destroying Giardia than the standard drug treatment (i.e. Flagyl). Amazingly, a kill rate of nearly 90% was achieved.

Treatment Protocol

Take a few drops of oil of oregano under the tongue twice daily. In addition, add a few drops to tomato juice or water and drink twice daily. For superior results, do a liver purge before consuming the oil. Mix a quarter cup of pure extra virgin olive oil with a few tablespoons of vinegar and drink. Follow one hour later with the oil of oregano. The liver flush will help purge the parasite from the biliary tracts in the liver. In addition, take Oregamax, three capsules twice daily.

Gum disease

Gum disease is defined as the degeneration of the structure and function of the gum tissue. Also known as periodontal disease, it afflicts tens of millions of Americans. In fact, dentists estimate that as many as 95% of Americans suffer from it.

Gum disease is largely due to poor diet and nutritional deficiency. The gums are rapidly growing tissues and are highly dependent upon a steady supply of nutrients for proper health. It is important to understand that gum disease is a dilemma of the Western world. Societies which thrive upon native diets consisting of a wide range of natural unprocessed foods are free of it. Civilized people have diseased gums. The main culprit is refined sugar. The consumption of processed nutrient-deprived foods is the major cause of gum disease.

Once the gums degenerate they are readily infected by a host of microbes. Infection of the gums is known as pyorrhea. Receding gums are defined as a recession of the gum tissue from the normal fit against the teeth. This structural deformity greatly increases the risk for pyorrhea by creating pockets along the gum-tooth interface.These pockets may readily become contaminated by food particles, which leads to microbial overgrowth. The microbes secrete various substances and waste products which further damage the gums and teeth.

Receding gums is strictly due to nutritional deficiency, although hormonal factors may be involved. Nutrients which help maintain normal gums and prevent recession include folic acid, riboflavin, vitamin C, bioflavonoids, vitamin A, vitamin K, calcium, phosphorus, and vitamin D. Healing and regenerating the gums involves taking the appropriate nutritional supplements as well as increasing the intake of the deficient nutrients through improved diet. There is enormous variability as to the degree to which an individual is deficient. To carefully determine the extent of your nutritional deficiencies, as well as find out how to correct them, see the Web site, NutritionTest.com.

Treatment protocol

Rub oil of oregano as needed upon all gum surfaces twice daily. Place a small amount on the toothbrush and use as a dentrifice. It may also be mixed with toothpaste. As an overnight treatment saturate a small piece of cotton with the oil; apply it high on the gum line and leave overnight.

Food poisoning

The term food poisoning is sort of a misnomer. The food doesn't usually cause the poisoning; it's the microbes that are the culprits. Thus, the more descriptive term would be "microbe poisoning."

Microbe poisoning of food is a major cause of ill health in America. The dilemma is so extensive that thousands of individuals are afflicted by acute food poisoning every day, meaning that the yearly victims number in the millions. The fact is the number of afflicted individuals contracting it on a yearly basis is so numerous that government organizations, such as the CDC, are unable to tabulate the count.

There are no dependable medical treatments for food-borne microbial infection; antibiotics are essentially impotent and often aggravate the infection. This illustrates the need for natural non-toxic agents for destroying the organisms. The U.S. FDA studied oil of oregano versus food poisoning germs. It killed every noxious germ against which it was tested. Thus, oil of oregano is a boon for treating food poisoning (see section "Diarrhea").

Treatment protocol

Take a few drops in juice or water as an internal antiseptic. Also, take it under the tongue, 2 or more drops as often as needed. Consume Oregamax, 3 to 4 capsules several times daily. If the diarrhea is severe, fill a gelatin capsule with the oil, and take one capsule twice daily. Continue treatment until symptoms of food poisoning are aborted. If the condition worsens, seek medical attention immediately.

Head lice

It is disconcerting to think that lice can infect humans, and yet, it happens to millions of individuals every day. The fact is humans are the primary host for this despised organism. The vast majority of victims are children attending public schools, however, adults are often infected as well. The infection usually begins in school age children as a result of poor hygiene, and it is quickly spread to other children in the school. The children then can spread the infection within the home, and the entire family may become infected.

Lice is the plural for louse, an organism possessing the medical name of Pediculus. This parasite is one of the few which has a specific predilection for humans. The parasites attach to the skin, hair, and clothes. They have a propensity for infecting hairy regions. They lay eggs virtually everywhere, but the primary repositories are skin, hair, clothes, and bedding. Not just a nuisance, lice may transmit serious diseases, including typhus, viral fevers, trench fever, and even the plague.

Treatment protocol

For hair infestation add one dropperful of oil of oregano to a tablespoon of shampoo. Wash hair thoroughly and let stand for several minutes; rinse to remove shampoo. As a body wash add a full dropper of oil of oregano to a handful of liquid soap; wash all body regions except genitals. For genital infection use a dilute solution to avoid burning sensation (use only one or two drops in a tablespoon of shampoo or liquid soap). Use a few drops in a small handful of liquid soap and wash gently; rinse thoroughly. Clothes and other inanimate objects, such as combs, hair dryers, and bedding, may become infested. For clothes and bedding add two or three droppers of oil of oregano to the wash cycle. For this purpose purchase the extra strength variety. For combs and other inanimate objects soak in hot water plus a drop or two of oil of oregano. Note: a specific formula researched and proven to kill lice is available. Scalp Clenz, manufactured by the North American Herb & Spice Company, is a combination of several anti-lice essential oils, with oregano oil as an active ingredient. It is completely non-toxic and safe for any age. Simply rub Scalp Clenz on the scalp; leave on as long as possible. Results are rapid, with only one or two applications necessary. This is a new product, so it must be ordered via mail order: call 1-800-243-5242.

Headaches

Essential oils have been used as headache cures for thousands of years. The use of oregano as a treatment for headaches dates to ancient Greece, where it was used internally and externally. It was also vaporized. The ancients found a connection between inhalation and a reduction in headache pain for a variety of essential oils.

The connection between essential oil vapors and headaches is explained anatomically. Smells are transmitted from the nose to the brain through a region which is essentially paper thin. Called the cribiform plate, this tiny bone is essentially the only barrier between the mucous membranes of the roof of the sinuses and brain tissue. Volatile components of essential oils readily traverse this barrier and exert their effects directly upon the brain. Oil of oregano is highly volatile, so it will exert therapeutic actions upon the brain through this mechanism. I have personally used the oil topically and via inhalation for headaches, finding it highly effective as well as exceptionally rapid in action.

Molds may provoke migraines. It is well known that molds produce a variety of alkaloids and other toxins, which may dramatically disrupt blood flow and cause inflammation within the organs. The toxic action of these mold-derived compounds can result in constriction of the blood vessels of the brain, depriving it of oxygen and nutrients: headaches may result. Oil of oregano kills mold, especially the type found in foods. This may explain the historical use of oregano oil and the crushed herb for headaches. Foods which may contain a high mold content include grains, cheese, vinegar, bakery, fruit, nuts, and fruit juices. Interestingly, cheese, which is produced through the action of molds, is one of the most common causes of migraines. The connection between various fermented foods and migraine headaches may be explained by residues of mold poisons, that is mycotoxins. As oil of oregano neutralizes mycotoxins on contact, in the event of a mold-induced migraine the relief may be profound.

Oil of oregano is a powerful anti-inflammatory agent, and this is largely why it is so effective for headaches. It helps reduce the inflammation in spastic muscles and decreases swelling in tissues such as the scalp, neck, and shoulder muscles, which often become inflamed during a headache.

Often, small discreet points of pain are palpable in various regions throughout the body during a headache crisis. These localized sites of pain are known as trigger points. When pressed with heavy pressure they exhibit pain, but this may also induce relief in the headache. They can be found in the scalp, neck, shoulders, and upper back. Interestingly, headache trigger points are also found in such seemingly remote locations as the hands, calves, and feet.

Mold toxicity is a virtual epidemic in modern society. Global warming has added to this crisis, as mold counts remain exceptionally high, even late in the seasons. What's more, the increasing incidence of sinus migraines may be attributed to mold, since these organisms readily infect the sinus cavities. If you suddenly develop a migraine, mold is a likely cause.

Case history: During a lecture I was giving on the powers of oil of oregano an attendee mentioned she was suffering from a severe migraine. She was a heavy grain eater, and I suspected mold intolerance. She was given a bottle of oil of oregano, which she rubbed externally on the temples and took a few drops several times under the tongue. Miraculously, the headache was eliminated within 15 minutes, and she was able to enjoy the rest of the lecture.

Treatment protocol

Rub oil of oregano liberally on inflamed neck and shoulders tissues. Massage a small amount into painful regions and trigger points in the scalp. Massage the feet with oil of oregano and rub into any sore spots/trigger points on the hands, neck, shoulders, and feet. Inhale the oil frequently. Take a few drops under the tongue as often as necessary, even every hour. Repeat these treatments until the pain is resolved. As a maintenance take oil of wild oregano under the tongue, 2 or 3 drops twice daily. Also, take Oregamax capsules, 2 capsules twice a day.

Hepatitis

Literally, this means inflammation of the liver. The liver inflammation may result from infection and/or toxicity. The majority of cases of hepatitis are caused by viral infections, although parasitic infestation of the liver may also lead to it. Furthermore, alcohol and drugs commonly induce hepatitis, as do a variety of environmental chemicals. Hundreds of prescription drugs can induce hepatitis. Some of the more common offenders include acetaminophen, birth control pills, antibiotics, cholesterol lowering drugs, and antifungal agents.

The medical profession regards hepatitis as incurable. Every year hundreds of thousands, perhaps millions, of Americans develop hepatitis; the American Liver Foundation estimated that some 350,000 Americans developed hepatitis B and C alone in 1995 and that this rate will rise significantly each year. Worldwide, hepatitis strikes some 200 million people per year, roughly five percent of the global population. It claims a greater number of lives per year than AIDS.

Several viruses from a variety of species may cause hepatitis, but the most common group are the herpetic viruses. The three primary species are known as hepatitis A, B, and C. The latter was formerly known as non-A non-B. There are also hepatitis D and E, the E type being common in underdeveloped countries. Recently, hepatitis G was discovered. Regarded as a mild type of hepatitis (in my view no type can be deemed mild), 1 to 2% of American adults are thought to be infected, which is a large number considering that most individuals are symptom free. At this rate of discovery the rest of the alphabet will soon be filled with variants of hepatitis.

It is important to realize that viral hepatitis is readily contracted by close human contact, that is it is usually transmitted via direct or indirect contact with human secretions and excrement. Examples of direct contact include failure to wash hands after changing diapers or using the restroom. From soiled hands the virus may be disseminated during food preparation or perhaps via seemingly innocuous contact such as hand shaking or touching inanimate objects. Hepatitis may also be transmitted sexually. This is one of the most common modes for transmitting hepatitis C infection. Direct contact can occur in hospitals, and health care practitioners are at high risk for infection. The usual source of infection is contaminated blood, with accidental injuries from needles or surgical accidents being common modes of transmission. Indirect contact includes contracting the infection by eating contaminated shellfish, which harbor the virus as a result of water polluted with human waste. Obviously, drug addicts who use contaminated needles have an exceptionally high rate of infection.

The majority of types of hepatitis are readily transmitted through sexual contact. While it has been poorly reported, this is one of the primary modes of transmission for hepatitis C. Thus, sexual promiscuity may readily lead to hepatitis.

Oil of oregano and the crushed wild herb are particularly valuable for infectious hepatitis. The fact is oil of oregano may prove lifesaving in the event of severe hepatitis. The volatile oil readily penetrates into the blood and is then carried to the liver tissue, where it exerts its antiseptic actions. To accelerate the absorption of the oil into the blood take oil of oregano with fatty meals.

Treatment protocol

Consume three or more drops of oil of oregano under the tongue twice daily. Take a few drops with meals in milk, juice, or water twice daily. Full fat milk is an ideal medium for the delivery of the active ingredients. Also, take Oregamax, three capsules two or three times daily. For tougher circumstances take the SuperStrength oil of oregano, three to five drops twice daily. Remember, the liver is capable of healing itself. The key is to cleanse it of impurities and destroy any noxious invaders.

Gene's powerdrops is one of the finest of all liver cleansing herbals. Made from wild vegetation, it is potent, but it is also completely safe. There is no chance for liver toxicity, in fact, the wild herbs and greens in the powerdrops greatly aid liver function. It is potent, so only small amounts are needed, like 5 to 10 drops once or twice daily. This is a highly specialized product, so it isn't available in stores. As it is made from wild greens found only in the most remote wilderness, only a limited supply is available. However, the powerdrops are perhaps the most powerful liver-regenerating herbal extract known. To order call 1-800-243-5242.

Hives

Hives are generally thought to be caused by allergic reactions. However, they can also be caused by infections, especially parasitic and/or fungal infections. Germs produce toxins, and when those toxins are absorbed into the blood, they may provoke hives. Certain foods may provoke hives. Common culprits include citrus fruit, legumes, and seafood. Food additives, like artificial colors and flavors, are also major instigators. In the event of infectious hives the germs must be destroyed for the hives to be eradicated. With food allergy-induced hives the allergenic foods must be removed from the diet.

Drugs also induce hives, in fact, they are one of the most common causes of this distressing complaint. Both prescription and non-prescription drugs may be the culprit. See your doctor for help in eliminating toxic drugs.

Treatment protocol

Rub the oil of oregano on any involved site. Also, take the oil under the tongue as often as needed. This helps immensely with the itching and swelling. Take Oregamax, two or more capsules twice daily. Unless you are allergic to bee stings for adrenal support take crude royal jelly, e.g. Royal Kick, two capsules twice daily.

Impetigo

This is an infection of the various layers of the skin, usually occurring on the face. It is caused by staph or strep. Impetigo is manifested by inflammation and redness of the skin along with crusting and pustule formation. The pustules become crusty and often burst, releasing an infectious solution. While adults may be afflicted, the usual victims are children, who develop a highly contagious form called impetigo cantagiosa.

If it is untreated, impetigo usually spreads aggressively throughout the skin, although the face and neck are the primary regions of infection. However, the bacteria is so contagious that merely touching the lesions and then touching another region spreads it. Rarely, the infection may become disseminated into the blood. The risk for spread is increased by certain drugs, particularly cortisone, aspirin, and non-steroidal anti-inflammatory agents such as ibuprofen. These drugs increase pathogenicity by impeding the normal immune response.

Recurrent infection may warn of an internal component, that is the infection may be housed within the body. Then, as a result of some immune disruptive factor, such as stress, drug therapy, antibiotics or poor diet, the strep or staph becomes activated and erupts in the skin.

Medical tests have proven that oil of oregano halts or impedes the growth of both staph and strep. According to a recent study published at Georgetown University even the drug resistant types succumb to its antiseptic powers. The oil also ameliorates the inflammation, rash, crusting, and irritation that typically occurs in impetigo. Taken internally, it aids in the eradication of staph and strep infections of the blood and/or internal organs.

Treatment protocol

Gently dab oil of oregano on all lesions with a saturated cotton ball. After application, discard cotton ball. Repeat several times daily. Be sure to wash hands thoroughly after touching lesions. Add oil of oregano to all pump soaps, and be sure to wash hands frequently, as this will help minimize the spread of infection. Also, take a few drops of oil of oregano twice daily in juice, milk, or water. Take Oregamax, three capsules twice daily.

Irritable bowel syndrome

Colonic disorders are incredibly common in Americans. Irritable bowel syndrome is represented by a variety of medical diagnoses, including colitis, Crohn's disease, spastic colon, and ulcerative colitis. Diseases of the colon are an utter plague of modern humanity, and they are exclusively due to errant diet.

The typical American diet creates great strain upon the colon. The colon thrives upon fiber, and the American diet is notoriously low in it. Most Americans are raised on foods which are highly processed and devoid of fiber. There is no fiber in soft drinks, bakery, cookies, white bread, pasta, pies, cakes, French fries, hamburgers, etc., and these are the types of foods that most people eat. Eating processed foods damages the colon wall: the longer the poor diet is followed the greater is the damage.

However, fiber is not the only nutrient lacking for colonic health. Certain nutrients are necessary for maintaining the health of the colon, including pantothenic acid, folic acid, vitamin B-12, vitamin A, vitamin D, vitamin K, magnesium, calcium, selenium, and potassium. Furthermore, a lack of healthy bacteria, particularly the Lactobacillus organisms, also places the colon at risk.

Once the colonic wall becomes damaged, it may be readily infected by a variety of organisms. The fact is infection is a major cause of colonic disease. This is why oil of oregano is so valuable as a treatment for this condition. It helps destroy the toxic microbes which damage the colon.

Parasitic infection is a common cause of irritable bowel syndrome. In fact, the illness may be precipitated after contraction of a parasite from contaminated food or water. Here again oil of oregano, as well as the crushed herb, is an ideal remedy, since it possesses significant antiparasitic actions.

The crushed spice, in the form of Oregamax, is an ideal herb for colonic disorders. Oregano spice aids digestion by enhancing the flow of digestive juices. It provides fiber, plus it is rich in minerals that aid intestinal function such as calcium, magnesium, potassium, and zinc. In particular, the high calcium and magnesium content helps relieve spasticity and cramps. The oily component of the herb contains terpenes and long chain alcohols, which help prevent allergic toxicity. It contains various essential oils, which ease spasticity and tension within the intestinal walls. Oregano spice is a versatile digestive tonic. Rhus coriaria, its companion herb, is a rich source of tannic, gallic, and malic acids. These substances aid colon health, because they are natural antiseptics. In particular, tannic acid exhibits significant antiparasitic and antifungal properties. Furthermore, these acids are astringents, meaning they help improve the tone of the colonic membranes.

Treatment protocol

Take a few drops of oil of oregano internally in juice or water (it blends exceptionally well in tomato or V-8 juice). The oil may also be used in a retention enema; in the event of parasitic infection add several drops to the enema bag and be sure to hold in the colon as long as possible. However, the OregaJuice, which is the water soluble extract of wild oregano, is the ideal type for enema administration. Add two or more ounces to each enema bag, and retain as long as possible. The Juice may be used by itself as an enema agent; simply fill the enema bag with it and squirt it in; retain as long as possible. A small amount of salt may also be added to this solution. For additional antiseptic power take Oreganol gelcaps, two caps twice daily. Take also Oregamax, three capsules with each meal.

Leg cramps

There are a number of causes of leg cramps, but the common factor is that they are due to a lack of blood flow in the muscles. When applied topically oil of oregano dramatically improves blood flow to muscles. The increase in circulation causes a greater amount of oxygen to be delivered. This increased amount of oxygen within the tissues nourishes the muscles, and the leg cramps are resolved.

Sore muscles also respond to the oregano prescription. The oil stimulates circulation to the sore or overused muscles, and this aids in rapid healing as well as in the removal of accumulated toxins. Furthermore, its deep antiinflammatory powers help reverse the toxic damage that occurs to muscles due to overexertion. Crude, wild oregano is a rich source of trace minerals. It is an excellent source of calcium and magnesium, both of which are needed for muscle contraction. A deficiency of these minerals may lead to leg cramps.

Treatment Protocol

Rub oil of oregano vigorously over spastic muscles until the cramps are halted. Muscle cramps may be a sign of calcium and magnesium deficiency. Take Oregamax as a natural calcium/magnesium supplement, 4 capsules three times daily. *Case history:* Mr. G. suddenly developed a nighttime foot cramp. He remembered he had read about the naturally occurring minerals in Oregamax; he took 2 capsules, and the foot cramp was eliminated in less than 4 minutes.

Nail fungus

Currently, there is an epidemic of fungal infections in Americans, and fungal nail infections are exceedingly common. Both fingernails and toenails may be affected, although toenail fungal infection is the most common type. Fungal infection of the nails is one of the most difficult of all disorders to cure. Recently, a number of oral medications have been promoted as effective cures, and, indeed, many of these medications eradicate nail fungus. However, all of these medications have the potential of causing significant toxicity, including liver damage.

Oil of oregano aids in the cure primarily through topical application, although internal consumption is necessary. The oil has a deep penetrating power, which aids in the destruction of nail fungus, since this fungus infects the root of the nail bed as well as the surface. Regarding essential oils, oil of oregano's ability to destroy nail fungus is unmatched.

Treatment protocol

Rub oil of oregano liberally into involved nails as often as possible. Take two or three drops under the tongue twice daily and/or take a few drops internally in milk, juice, or water. Also take Oregamax, three capsules twice daily. Be sure also to reduce sugar intake.

Paronychia

This is a type of infection of the tissues surrounding the nail and nail bed. The skin directly surrounding the nail becomes infected.

As there is very little space between the skin and the nail bed when the region becomes swollen and inflamed, the infection results in great pain and pressure.

Paronychia is often caused by Candida infection, although infections by staph and strep are other prominent causes. The risk for infection is increased by poor hygiene and constant immersion of the hands in water or soapy water. Contact of the hands with toxic chemicals also increases the risk.

Antibiotics are often prescribed for treating this condition. However, the problem is that antibiotics only kill bacteria, and Candida albicans is immune to them. Oil of oregano is the ideal substance to use, since it is active against all of the organisms which cause paronychia, plus it aids in the relief of the pain, pressure, and swelling.

Treatment protocol

Apply oil of oregano directly to the involved region several times daily. Take oil of oregano internally, two or more drops twice daily in juice or water. Also, take Oregamax, three capsules twice daily.

Peptic ulcer

Ulcers occur either in the stomach or upper intestine, i.e. the duodenum. The term "peptic" defines both of these types of ulcers. For decades the medical profession has assumed that peptic ulcers are due to excess stomach acid, which eats away at the gut lining. This view has now been proven erroneous; for instance, peptic ulcers are equally common in people who have low amounts of stomach acid. Interestingly, both stomach cancer and stomach ulcers occur most commonly in people who have no stomach acid, a condition known as *achlorhydria.* The cause of stomach ulcers came to light recently after decades of ignorance. During the 1980s when analyzing the tissue found in ulcers researchers made a crucial discovery: that the ulcers were infected by large amounts of a microbe known as *Helicobacter pylori.* Ulcers occur primarily in two regions: the stomach and duodenum (upper small intestine). Incredibly, 90% of all duodenal ulcers and 60% or more of stomach ulcers are infected with Helicobacter. This explains why stomach ulcers are more common in individuals lacking stomach acid, since hydrochloric acid is the most potent antiseptic known. Impressively, the researchers determined that if the organism was destroyed through antibiotic therapy, the ulcers healed completely.

Oil of oregano is highly active against the stomach ulcer bacteria. The organism is relatively difficult to destroy, so treatment may need to be prolonged. Destruction of the organism is critical; stomach infection by Helicobacter pylori increases the risk for gastric cancer by some 600%.

Treatment protocol

Take a few drops of oil of oregano by mouth two or three times daily. Mix in juice or water. Also, take Oregamax, three capsules 3 times daily on an empty stomach. <u>*Case history*</u>: Mrs. Z. had suffered with a seemingly incurable case of Heliobacter infection for several years. Antibiotics failed to eradicate the germ. She took the Oreganol oil of oregano as well as the capsules. Within one month she was cured of the infection and all symptoms were resolved.

Pneumonia

This is the most severe of all lung infections and is a major cause of death in the United States, particularly in the elderly. It is defined simply as infection of the lung tissue, that is the lobes of the lungs. If severe, the entire lung becomes filled with infection and inflammation. The result is severe chest and back pain, shortness of breath, cough, fever, chills, and malaise. The temperature may reach as high as 105 degrees. Dehydration is a common consequence of the high temperature, and, thus, it is important to drink large quantities of fluids. Pneumonia is a frequent complication of invasive procedures, particularly surgery, and is the most common cause of post surgical mortality.

Pneumonia may be caused by viruses, bacteria, and fungi, although parasites may also be involved. Viruses are responsible for the greatest number of cases, especially in children. Regardless of the culprit cause oil of oregano is an invaluable treatment. It possesses antiseptic powers against virtually all pneumonia-causing organisms. The oil, as well as Oregamax, helps induce sweating, and this aids in breaking the high temperature and accelerating the recovery. Furthermore, oil of oregano helps thin mucous and opens clogged lung/nasal passages, and this aids in relief of cough as well as shortness of breath.

Treatment protocol

Inhale the oil of oregano directly from the bottle as often as possible. Take a few drops under the tongue twice daily. Rub a generous amount of the oil on the upper chest and along the spine over the upper and mid back. Take Oregamax, 3 capsules three times daily.

Poison ivy, poison oak, and poison sumac

Usually, when a rash occurs from skin contact with plants, the assumption is that it is poison ivy. While this is the most common cause of plant associated rash there are dozens of other plants which may cause serious skin rashes. Poison oak and sumac are close cousins of poison ivy and are probably the second most common cause of plant-induced allergic rash. A partial list of other plants which may cause immediate rash when in contact with the skin include stinging nettle, chrysanthemum, citrus rind, garlic, onion, tomato, strawberry, cayenne, and kiwi fruit. Regarding edible plants some individuals may develop a rash merely from handling the foods or their juices; even the inhalation of aroma may provoke an allergic response in highly sensitive individuals.

The skin toxicity of the poison ivy family is the result of a noxious plant resin, which the plant contains in large amounts. This resin aggressively irritates the skin and is readily spread. Being a resin, it clings to the skin and is difficult to remove with normal washing.

Oil of oregano dissolves the resin, allowing it to be removed from the body by normal washing. The oil also halts the inflammation and swelling that typically occurs as a result of allergic reactions. Furthermore, it rapidly relieves itching and, thus, helps prevent the spread of the rash.

Treatment protocol

Gently apply oil of oregano over the involved region(s) several times daily. Add the oil to all soaps when washing. Also, take 2 or more drops under the tongue as needed. The oral dosing also helps relieve the itching.

Psoriasis

Up to 3% of people living in Westernized countries suffer from this unsightly condition, a disease which only occurs in "modernized" countries. Medical treatment for this illness has been largely futile, despite the application of a wide range of treatments, many of them bizarre and/or toxic. Unfortunately, the majority of psoriasis victims suffer continuous disability despite medical treatment.

One reason for the poor results is that physicians believe that the disease has no known cause or cure. However, there is evidence against this conventional view. Few people realize that psoriasis, as has been documented by Dr. Rosenburg and colleagues of the University of Tennessee, is caused largely by a fungal infection. Bacterial infection is another major cause. Furthermore, hormonal disturbances, notably hypothyroidism and adrenal disorders, play a significant role in the genesis of this condition.

According to Rosenburg, whose work was published in *Archives of Dermatology*, the fungus which causes psoriasis is located certainly in the lesions themselves, but it goes beyond this. It appears that the reservoir for the organism is the intestinal tract, from which it is seeded to the skin. Thus, in order to resolve psoriasis, antifungal treatment must be aimed both internally and externally. In medicine this treatment is also utilized; ketoconazole, an antifungal drug, is the treatment of choice for scalp psoriasis.

Sugar feeds fungus. The majority of individuals with psoriasis are sugar addicts. Thus, a low sugar or sugar free diet would aid in the cure. The diet should be rich in protein, natural fats, and low in sugar. Avoid all sugary foods, such as candy, soft drinks, pastries, ice cream, and puddings, as well as starchy foods, such as potatoes, grains, and pasta. Instead, eat low sugar fruits and vegetables such as cantaloupe, strawberries, papaya, kiwi, watermelon, dark greens, red sweet peppers, celery, broccoli, cabbage, brussels sprouts, turnips, radishes, green peppers, and tomatoes. However, a diet which restricts even fruit might be necessary in the early phases of treatment. For instance, for the first 90 days eat primarily meat, fish, eggs, milk products, and vegetables, limiting the fruit intake to no more than one serving daily.

Oil of oregano is highly effective for psoriasis. It gives significant relief to the common symptoms of soreness, itching, inflammation, and swelling. Furthermore, because of its antifungal and antibacterial powers it outright eradicates the lesions. Internal consumption offers the best results. This is because the fungi and bacteria which cause the disease live deep within the tissues, like the internal linings of the gut, the bladder, kidney, vaginal tract, etc. Thus, for a thorough cure to result they must be destroyed from within.

Treatment protocol

Internal consumption is more reliable than topical application, since the fungus originates within the tissues, particularly the gut. Take 5 or more drops of oil of oregano under the tongue and/or in juice two or three times daily. For extra antifungal effects take Oreganol gelcaps, two caps twice daily with meals. Apply the oil twice daily to psoriatic lesions. Take Oregamax, three capsules two or three times daily. For difficult cases take the SuperStrength oil of oregano, 5 to 10 drops under the tongue twice daily. Be persistent; this is the only hope you have.

Prostate disorders

There has been a massive rise in the incidence of prostate cancer in recent years. Currently, it is the second leading cause of cancer deaths among men.

Contrary to popular belief prostate cancer is far from a necessary consequence of a long life in the modern world. In other words, it can be prevented through dietary and nutritional means.

Infection is one of the most common provocative factors with prostate disorders. The prostate gland is a reservoir for the development of infections, and usually, they are of a sexually transmitted nature. Poor hygiene may also be a factor, and E. coli infection is a relatively common cause of prostatitis. Other organisms which readily infect the prostate include Chlamydia, gonococcus (i.e. gonorrhea), proteus, staph, and Candida albicans.

When prostatic infection or inflammation becomes extreme, a variety of symptoms result. These include low back pain, reduced urinary stream, dribbling of urine, incomplete emptying of urine, pain upon urination, and burning upon urination. Oil of oregano is useful in prostate problems, especially those caused by infection. Its deep penetrating powers and antiinflammatory action make it invaluable for easing disconcerting lower back pain. Taken orally, it aids in the eradication of prostatic infections, which are notoriously difficult to cure.

Treatment protocol

Take a few drops of oil of oregano under the tongue once or twice daily. Rub the oil on the lower back just above the sacrum once or twice daily. Take Oregamax, three capsules twice daily; consume it more often during an acute attack, i.e. three or four times daily. Note: the wild oregano products work better if combined with a highly touted prostate health supplement known as Pumpkinol. This is the original crude form of pumpkinseed oil derived from a special type of pumpkin which grows in the Alpine region of Europe. Crude pumpkinseed oil has been used as a prostate tonic for hundreds of years and offers both potency and safety. In 17th century Europe the crude pumpkinseed oil was deemed so valuable that its sale as a food was prohibited and, instead, it was sold in pharmacies (as a medicine). The Pumpkinol is unique, because it is fortified with edible essential plant oils known to support the health of the urinary tract. Take two or more tablespoons of Pumpkinol daily. Check your health food store or call 1-800-243-5242.

Pruritus (itchy skin)

Oil of oregano may effectively resolve itching, especially if it is due to allergic reactions. The oil is particularly effective for remedial action against itching due to direct contact of the skin with poisonous compounds such as the resins of poisonous plants, soap residues, petrochemicals, insecticides, herbicides, and metals. Since it is an aggressive solvent, it helps neutralize various poisons and, thus, reverses skin toxicity.

Allergic reactions are another common cause of itching, and often the itch is associated with a rash. Virtually any food may cause an allergic itch and/or rash, however, the most common culprits include citrus fruit, wheat, milk products, shrimp, potatoes, berries, spices, and tomatoes. A variety of food-borne chemicals may cause allergic reactions, and the list includes MSG, sulfites, NutraSweet, nitrates, nitrites, food dyes, and artificial flavors.

Pruritus may also be a sign of serious disease. A partial list of such illnesses includes hepatitis, cancer, kidney failure, liver failure, and internal fungal infection. In these instances the pruritus may be due to toxic overload of the liver. If the liver is cleansed of impurities, the pruritus may be cured.

Oil of wild oregano is active against allergic rash, as it reduces inflammation while blocking the itch. When taken internally, the oil and, particularly, the crushed herb help neutralize food allergy reactions. However, the oil is also active against the pruritus of serious diseases, as it helps cleanse the lymph and skin of poisons, while boosting liver function. Gene's powerdrops, the wild greens variety, is an excellent addition to the wild oregano treatment. The powerdrops help purge the liver of toxins by increasing the flow of poisons through the bile. A cleansing response is normal.

Treatment protocol

Apply oil of oregano to itchy area. Do not apply large amounts to the face, as this may result in a strong burning sensation. Repeat as necessary. If itching or rash fail to improve or if the condition worsens, discontinue use. Also, if the itching is due to chronic disease take Gene's powerdrops, wild greens formula, 5 or more drops twice daily. The powerdrops are a rare nutritional supplement, so they may not be available commercially. To order call 1-800-243-5242.

Radiation injury/burns

Radiation destroys human tissue, both internally and externally. The vast majority of radiation burns occur as a result of radiation therapy for cancer.

The problem with radiation therapy is that it destroys both healthy and cancerous tissues. If the treatment is applied repeatedly, severe burns of the skin may result. Radiation burns often result in open wounds, which readily become infected by bacteria and/or fungi. Candida albicans infection is a common secondary infection in radiation wounds.

If wound healing is slow, this may warn of significant infection in the wound as well as nutritional deficiency. Radiation destroys a wide range of nutrients. When radiation treatments are applied a massive stress reaction occurs. This is associated with the depletion of the body's nutrient reserves. Thus, widespread deficiencies of vitamins, minerals, and amino acids readily develop. To speed the healing of radiation-damaged tissue take supplemental dosages of vitamins A, C, and D as well as riboflavin, pantothenic acid, folic acid, vitamin E, zinc, and selenium. Take at least 400 mcg of organically bound selenium daily. Aloe vera cream or gel also greatly aids in the healing of radiation burns.

Oil of oregano helps prevent the development of infection in radiation-induced burns or ulcers. Plus, it speeds healing of the wounds. A combination of the oil plus pure aloe vera is an ideal topical anti-radiation cure.

Treatment protocol

Apply oil of oregano to the burn site; repeat application two or three times daily. Take Oregamax, three capsules two or three times daily until the lesions heal. Afterwards, use a maintenance dose of two capsules daily.

Ringworm

Ringworm is a fungal infection of the skin. Virtually any part of the skin may be attacked, although the most prominent sites include the scalp, face, back, chest, abdomen, legs, and arms.

Ringworm is caused by a fungus known as *tinea*. This organism has a predilection for the skin and, in fact, thrives upon a protein in the skin known as keratin. It lives on the keratin in the dead cells that are shed by the skin every day. Tinea is readily destroyed by oil of oregano, in fact, the organism is no match for it. Researchers have discovered that oil of oregano is directly toxic to tinea, and, when evaluated in the laboratory, it totally destroyed all species of the organism. If the oil is applied regularly, a complete resolution of ringworm should be evident in as little as a week.

Treatment protocol

Rub oil of oregano on the affected region twice daily. Take Oregamax crude wild oregano capsules, three caps twice daily. Also, take a few drops of the oil once or twice daily in juice or water.

Rosacea

This is a bizarre type of skin rash that occurs primarily on the face, specifically on and about the nose. The illness affects the sebaceous glands, which become red, inflamed, and infected.

For years the medical profession has maintained that there is no cause nor cure for rosacea. However, new evidence is to the contrary: infection seems to be the likely culprit. According to Dr. Mark Dahl, chairman of the department of dermatology at the University of Minnesota Medical School, the lesions of virtually all rosacea patients are infected by a parasite. Incredibly, the parasite is a type of mite known as *Demodex*, a genus of mites that infest the hair follicles and sebaceous ducts. The mites are found normally on skin. However, in rosacea they are found in vastly increased numbers. Other research points to internal infection as a factor. As published in *Family Practice News* in 1996 Helicobacter pylori, a bacteria which infects the inner linings of the stomach, may also be a factor. Apparently, the organism secretes a toxin which causes the pattern of inflammation and redness typically seen in rosacea. According to the researchers when the organism is destroyed by antibiotics, the rosacea disappears.

Oil of oregano kills mites. Plus, it reduces the inflammation and swelling associated with skin infections. Thus, it is the ideal remedy for this condition.

Treatment protocol

Use the oil of oregano aggressively by taking it internally. Topical application is secondary. Take three or more drops twice daily under the tongue, along with wild oregano oil gelcaps (Oreganol), two capsules twice daily. Apply oil of oregano directly to the involved sites once or twice daily. Also, take Oregamax, three capsules twice daily. Note: it is important to be patient, that is don't get discouraged. As it often takes several years for rosacea to develop, it may take several weeks before improvement occurs. To speed the process use the SuperStrength oil of oregano, two or more drops under the tongue twice daily.

Scabies

Scabies is a parasitic infection of the skin caused by a mite known as *Sarcoptes scabiei*. The mite is rather large and causes skin burrows, which are readily seen.

Infection is most prominent about the genitals, finger webs, elbows, wrists, belt line, thighs, nipples (in women), lower abdomen, and lower buttocks. Facial infection may occur in infants. Any skin fold is a likely site of infection. Scabies mites thrive in moist regions. Areas where sweat or moisture accumulate are vulnerable.

In North America scabies usually occurs as an outbreak in public institutions such as schools, dormitories, military bases, and similar facilities. This is because it is readily spread by mass human contact and as a result of poor hygiene. However, it may also be contracted during travel in third world countries, where it is endemic.

Sexual contact is a primary mode of transmission. The parasite may be found on underwear, dirty sheets, or other inanimate objects. However, intimate contact is the means by which it is rapidly spread. Cats and dogs may also carry it, and it can spread to humans from them.

Once the mite is in contact with the skin, it burrows into the flesh in order to feed. Infection is rarely noticed right away, in fact, it may take weeks before symptoms occur. The primary symptom is severe itching and rash.

Scabies is highly contagious, and an unsuspecting individual may contract it sexually as well as from inanimate objects. To halt the spread the organism and its eggs must be entirely destroyed in and on the body as well as on bedding, clothes, or other objects.

The current medical treatment is the application of insecticide cream to the skin. According to the CDC the entire body is to be lathered with a solution of Lindane, a potent insecticide. The insecticide must remain on the skin for at least 8 hours before rinsing. Usually, the scabies mite will be killed. Repeated applications are not uncommon. Obviously, this is a potentially dangerous treatment, and a certain degree of tissue damage will result.

The use of insecticide is unnecessary, because oil of oregano destroys the scabies mite. The fact is the oil is an outright cure for this disconcerting condition.

Treatment protocol

Apply oil of oregano to involved regions. Cover the entire body from head to toe with a light film of the oil. To stretch the oil dilute one part oil of oregano to two parts olive oil. Repeat application to involved sites only. This procedure may be followed on a daily basis until the infection is resolved. Soak all potentially infected clothes, bedding, and articles in a solution of hot water and oil of oregano. Add two droppers of the oil to a gallon of water; let all infected items soak overnight in the solution before washing. For difficult or extreme cases use the SuperStrength oil of oregano.

Shingles

This feared disease is caused by a type of herpes virus, the same one that causes chicken pox. The virus is actually contracted early in life, perhaps as chicken pox, and hides in the nerve sheath and brain tissue. There it remains dormant unless activated. Forces which activate the virus include trauma, severe stress, nutritional deficiency, and certain drugs. In particular, cortisone, whether applied topically or internally, often provokes attacks of shingles.

Shingles is among the most painful and debilitating of all illnesses. This is because the virus directly invades and damages the nerve tissue. If left untreated, the virus may invade the internal organs, which can result in death. Oil of oregano and the crushed herb should be taken internally to halt the growth of this life threatening virus. The SuperStrength oil is the ideal one to use for topical application. It is 300% stronger and, thus, offers a higher degree of deep penetrating powers. *Case history:* While lecturing in Canada, I met a women who had suffered from post-herpetic neuralgia for several months. Drugs offered no relief for her pain. I mentioned the powers of SuperStrength oil of oregano. She rubbed the SuperStrength on the painful region that night. For the first time in months she slept well. By the next morning she was nearly pain free. Regular use of the SuperStrength has eliminated the pain.

Treatment protocol

Apply the regular oil of oregano or the SuperStrength variety directly to the involved sites; repeat application as often as necessary to ease pain and inflammation. Take a few drops of the oil under the tongue or in juice or water twice daily.

Sinusitis

Millions of Americans suffer from sinus problems. Symptoms such as post nasal drip, hayfever, and runny nose (i.e. rhinitis) have become the plague of modern humanity. This is readily apparent from viewing television, with its incessant ads for sinus medications as well as by viewing the typical pharmacy counters, which are filled with sinus remedies.

Defined as inflammation of the sinus cavities, sinusitis may be caused by a variety of factors. The most prominent causes are food allergy reactions, inhalant allergies, and infection. Few people realize that dietary habits are intimately involved in causing sinus conditions. Usually, when the sinuses are inflamed, it is assumed that it is an inhalant problem, like hayfever or an infection. Yet, sinusitis commonly results from a toxic reaction to food or beverage, and infection, as well as inhalant allergies, must be regarded as secondary causes.

Recent studies performed at the prestigious Mayo Clinic have seemingly defined the cause of chronic sinusitis: mold infestation. The researchers found some 40 different types of molds growing in victims' sinuses. The conclusion was that the molds were the cause of a wide range of sinus symptoms, including runny nose, post nasal drip, acute sinus infections, and stuffy sinuses.

Oil of oregano is a type of natural sinus medicine. It helps open clogged sinus passages, while thinning mucous as well as halting excessive mucous secretion. Oil of oregano also helps minimize the toxicity of allergic reactions. Yet, its greatest power is due to the fact that it kills molds and other sinus invaders outright.

The value of this oil in halting sinus attacks, hayfever, and rhinitis is stupendous. I have observed fits of sneezing and massive allergic attacks halted in a matter of seconds after administrating the oil. Years of sinus congestion are obliterated overnight. Put simply, oil of oregano and the crushed herb in the form of Oregamax have produced the best therapeutic response I have ever seen for the treatment of this condition.

Treatment protocol

Inhale the oil frequently to help open clogged passages. Place a drop or two of oil of oregano on the skin next to the nose for a more direct effect. Consume it under the tongue, three or more drops twice daily. Take Oregamax, two capsules twice daily, until the condition improves. As a maintenance take a drop or two daily under the tongue along with one or two Oregamax capsules.

Sore throat

There is nothing worse than a horrible sore throat. Traditional medicines are relatively ineffective in relieving pain and soreness. Usually, the affected individual suffers several days of excruciating pain, and antibiotics offer little or no relief: enter oregano oil. When applied directly upon the throat, it rapidly eliminates pain and inflammation, plus it quickly destroys the causative organism.

Sore throat may be caused by a variety of microbes, including bacteria, viruses, and yeasts. Assuming that it is bacterial is the mistake that is usually made. If the sore throat is bacterial in origin, antibiotics may be helpful, but, if it is caused by viral or yeast infection, antibiotics will only aggravate the problem. The unique benefit of oil of oregano is that it is useful for sore throat regardless of the microbial cause. This makes it invaluable particularly for families with children and/or adolescents, because they develop a wide range of upper respiratory tract infections. Furthermore, children in particular are highly vulnerable to the toxic effects of antibiotics and can, in fact, develop chronic sore throats as a result of persistent antibiotic therapy.

Treatment protocol

Since it is an edible spice extract, oil of wild oregano is completely safe: even for children. Add a few drops of oil of oregano to salt water and gargle several times daily. Take two or three drops of the oil under the tongue twice daily. Apply the oil directly to the back of the throat. Also, take Oregamax, three capsules three times daily.

Spinal infection

The spinal column is readily infected by a wide range of germs. The germs usually infect the inner fluid of the spine, known as the cerebrospinal fluid. However, germs may infect the spinal bone marrow as well as the spinal muscles. Spinal infections are becoming increasingly common. Causative organisms include meningococcus, staph, strep, tubercular bacteria, molds, fungi, and viruses, including the herpes virus.

Treatment protocol

Rub the oil of oregano vigorously (SuperStrength is the best variety) over the spinal column. Take oil of oregano under the tongue, 5 or more drops twice daily or two Oreganol gelcaps twice daily. The oil of oregano rub is best applied after a bath or shower. Note: an intense heat sensation after application is normal.

Sports injuries

You don't have to be injury prone to become injured in sports. It automatically happens, especially in combative sports such as football, wrestling, basketball, and hockey.

Athletes frequently suffer soft tissue injuries, which means trauma to the skin, fatty membranes, cartilage, tendons, muscles, and ligaments. These injuries may be open wounds or, more commonly, blunt injury or internal damage, including bruises, strains, sprains, contusions, pulled muscles, or torn ligaments and muscles. All of these injuries have one thing in common: pain and inflammation.

Fungal infection is common in athletes. Fungi abound in public environments, and infection may be readily contracted by contact of the bare skin on virtually any surface. Thus, athlete's foot and jock itch are epidemic in athletes. Oil of oregano outright destroys skin fungus, especially athlete's foot fungus. Furthermore, skin fungal infection can be prevented even in the volatile athletic environment, if the oil is regularly applied on vulnerable regions such as the groin, feet, and hands.

Oil of oregano is a versatile remedy for the athlete and has utility for a wide range of athletic injuries. A partial list of its applications include sprains, pulled muscles, torn muscles, ligamentous injuries, leg cramps, muscle aches, tendonitis, bursitis, carpal tunnel syndrome, neuritis, warts, bacterial infections, contusions, cuts, abrasions, and shin splints.

Oil of oregano is exceptionally useful for athletic trauma. It possesses potent anti-inflammatory action, and it deeply penetrates the tissues. Because of its penetrating power, it accelerates the healing of various traumatic injuries, while reducing and/or eliminating the pain. One reason it halts pain is that the oil contains a natural anesthetic. Its pronounced anti-pain actions make it the ideal athletic rub.

Treatment protocol

Rub the oil gently on the involved region. Repeat application several times daily until improvement occurs. Then, apply at least twice daily for inducing rapid healing. If rash or irritation occurs, discontinue use. Make your own athletic rub by mixing a liberal amount of oil of oregano into a solid fat such as lanolin or cocoa butter. Apply as needed. A special type of oil of oregano-based pain reliever is available. Called Pain-eez, this is a combination of several potent herb/spice extracts. It is remarkably effective. For severe pain gently apply Pain-eez as often as needed (usually only one or two applications are necessary). It is especially valuable for athletic injuries. However, the oil of oregano is by itself effective, as is illustrated by this case history: Mr. C. had a major accident: he dropped a 50 pound brick on his foot. Immediately, his wife rubbed the oil of oregano on the foot and took Mr. C. to the doctor. X-rays discovered a severe fracture, but what most astounded the doctor was the fact that despite pressing on the region there was no pain or swelling.

Stomach infection (Helicobacter pylori)

Researchers have clearly shown that infection is a major cause of chronic stomach disorders. Australian physicians were the first to prove that stomach ulcers, as well as chronic stomach pain, are largely due to infection by a bizarre bacteria known as Helicobacter pylori. This germ is able to evade the normal defenses of the stomach, for instance, stomach acid, and grow within the stomach walls. The infestation results in a wide range of disorders, including stomach pain, bloating, persistent heartburn, stomach ulcers, and, if prolonged, stomach cancer.

Oil of oregano is a potent antiseptic, which means it kills a wide range of germs. It sterilizes septic water. Cornell University reports that no germs resist its antiseptic powers.

Treatment protocol

Take oil of wild oregano under the tongue, 2 to 5 drops twice daily. Also, take Oreganol gelcaps, 1 or 2 capsules twice daily. If desired, drink the Juice of Oregano, a potent water-soluble tonic, one ounce twice daily.

Tick-borne illness

Diseases caused by ticks have reached epidemic proportions in the United States. Lyme disease is the most commonly occurring type followed by Rocky Mountain Spotted Fever and Ehrlichiosis. All of these diseases are caused by different organisms, and these organisms are transmitted directly to humans through the bites of ticks.

Lyme disease has captured national attention. It is an infection caused primarily by the bite of the deer tick, an organism which is so small that it may not be seen. This makes the diagnosis difficult, because the tick may infect the individual and become removed while never being discovered.

Lyme disease may present as little more than an odd circular rash or perhaps a mild feverish disorder which is readily disregarded. Other vague symptoms include headache, stiff neck, fatigue, drowsiness, jaw pain, stiff muscles/joints, chills, and fever. As a result of the evasive nature of the syndrome the infection is rarely caught early enough so that the proper medical treatment can be promptly administered (the cure being tetracycline or perhaps oregano oil), and this may result in serious disease. The Lyme organism, a spirochete with highly invasive powers, may infest virtually any organ of the body, causing extensive tissue damage—perhaps death. It has a particular affinity for nervous tissue, and loves to invade the brain and spinal column. Acute Lyme-induced illnesses which may lead to death include hepatitis, meningitis, and encephalitis. However, usually infected individuals develop a wide range of chronic ailments, including neuritis, arthritis, cardiomyopathy, heart failure, chronic fatigue syndrome, fibromyalgia, and neurological disorders.

Oil of oregano is an ideal antiseptic for combating tick-borne infections. Ticks transmit a wide range of poisonous microbes, not just the Lyme spirochete. This illustrates the need for a broad spectrum antiseptic capable of killing whatever nasty microbes the ticks might inject.

The tick's secretions are highly infective, and this is another reason oil of oregano is lifesaving. The oil helps sterilize the tick itself as well as its excrement and secretions.

Treatment protocol

Oil of oregano destroys ticks outright. If the tick is still attached, saturate it and the bite site with oil of oregano. Also, saturate a cotton ball and cover the tick; it should die promptly, that is within minutes. If possible, seek medical aid in removing the tick, or, if you are certain it is dead, remove it yourself with a tweezers. Be sure no remnants of the tick remain. Take a few drops of oil of oregano under the tongue twice daily and consume a few drops internally for at least one week in order to prevent the tick-borne microbe from gaining a foothold. Rub the oil on the spine once or twice daily. Also, consume Oregamax, three capsules twice daily. In addition, tetracycline therapy may be necessary, but this is useful only in the early stages. If you develop any unusual symptoms occurring within one month of a tick bite, seek medical attention immediately.

Thrush

This is the older medical term for yeast infection of the mouth. Now it is known as oral candidiasis. Thrush occurs when Candida albicans invades the mucous membranes of the mouth and/or throat.

It is totally abnormal to have thrush. In fact, the development of this condition may be a warning of severe immune depression.

It may be one of the first warning signs of AIDS.

Babies may develop thrush, but this is not usually a signal of AIDS. They develop it because their immune systems are immature and they cannot fight the yeast. Mothers may be the source. Babies may actually contract the infection from mothers as a result of passage through the birth canal. However, babies can be readily cured of this infection through antifungal medicines or, preferably, oil of oregano. In an adult thrush warns of AIDS or other serious forms of immunosuppression. Regardless of the cause oil of oregano is the most potent anti-thrush natural substance known.

Treatment protocol

Gargle with oil of oregano by adding a few drops in salt water. Flush the mouth with this solution several times daily. Apply the oil directly upon the gums and throughout the oral cavity. Also, take a few drops under the tongue twice daily. Take Oregamax, three capsules two or three times daily. For babies simply dilute the oil by adding one or two drops to a teaspoon of extra virgin olive oil and apply directly to the involved sites. Repeat two or three times daily until lesions are cleared.

Toothache

What fear the movies have created about having a toothache; they picture a man walking about in utter pain with an ice pack on his face. Have no fear, because oil of oregano can halt toothache pain rapidly and thoroughly.

Toothache is almost always caused by infection of the tooth, dentin, and, particularly, nerve root. Aching of the teeth, a milder condition, may be caused by a deficiency of calcium and magnesium or, more likely, a vitamin D deficiency. The latter is required for the deposition of calcium and magnesium into the enamel.

Oil of oregano is highly useful for this condition, largely because of its immense penetrating power. Its active ingredients are capable of penetrating the enamel, so that its powers can reach exactly where they are needed: the tooth socket and root. Plus, it is highly germicidal. A study performed by Weber State University determined that oil of oregano outright destroyed oral pathogens.

Treatment protocol

Apply the oil directly to the involved tooth or teeth several times daily. Or, saturate a piece of cotton with the oil and wedge it between cheek and gum at the involved region. May be applied as often as needed.

Tuberculosis

Tuberculosis is an infection caused by a bacteria known medically as *Mycobacterium tuberculosis.* This bacteria has a propensity for infecting the lungs, but it may also infect a variety of other organs, including the kidneys, spleen, intestines, nervous system, bones, endocrine glands, and skin.

It was believed that tuberculosis had been cured through the improvement in sanitation and through the administration of certain antibiotics. However, the disease has returned with a ferocity. The fact is tuberculosis is notoriously difficult to cure by any means. One of the reasons is because of the deep seated nature of the infection. Mycobacteria infect tissue regions, such as the deep recesses of the lungs, the spinal cord, the brain, the inner linings of the intestine, and the joints, where it may be difficult for the medication to penetrate. Plus, the mycobacteria are bizarre organisms, which lack the typical bacterial cell wall and, thus, are more readily able to evade immune defenses.

Oil of oregano is an ideal remedy for tuberculosis. When inhaled, it possesses a unique ability to penetrate lung tissue. When taken internally, it penetrates into the deep recesses of the internal organs, including the lungs, where the microbes readily hide. Taken continuously, it will greatly aid in eradicating this life-threatening condition.

Treatment protocol

Deeply inhale oregano oil several times daily. Place a small amount about the nose three times daily to ensure maximum inhalation. Fill a gelatin capsule with the oil and take one or two capsules daily with meals. Take also Oregamax, three capsules two or three times daily. Continue treatment for several weeks and/or months, if necessary. For persistent cases take the SuperStrength oil of oregano, 10 or more drops under the tongue twice daily. Be sure to get plenty of sunlight, since ultraviolet rays are highly toxic to the TB bacteria. Also, drink two ounces of Juice of Oregano twice daily. In the 17th century the juice was used as a TB therapy.

Varicose veins

A type of degenerative disease of the circulatory system, varicose veins are extremely common in Americans, afflicting nearly one of three individuals. In order to understand this condition it is important to review the function and structure of the veins. The purpose of the veins is to return blood from the periphery of the body back to the heart. They do this essentially by pumping the blood upwards towards the heart. The veins are normally highly elastic, that is they can expand and contract. They also contain valves, which aid in advancing the blood to the chest. For a variety of reasons, including nutritional deficiency, the walls and valves of the veins degenerate, that is they lose their elasticity. No drugs are available to treat this condition, and, although surgery is regarded as a potential treatment, it is a last resort.

When the vessel walls and valves degenerate, the veins lose their elasticity. Then, they bulge and collapse. This leads to a pooling of blood. The pooled blood causes pressure and/or pain.

Oil of oregano is an ideal treatment for the symptoms of this condition. Because of its penetrating antiinflammatory actions, it helps reduce the swelling, irritation, and pain associated with varicose veins. For determining the role of nutritional deficiency see the web site, NutritionTest.com.

Treatment protocol

Apply the oil directly to the swollen or painful varicosities. Follow the vein up and down, and apply the oil to visible portions. Repeat the application morning and night. If redness or inflammation occurs, discontinue use. Usually, improvement in the swelling and pain may be observed immediately after application. Also, take Oregamax crushed wild oregano capsules, two caps twice daily.

Venomous bites

There are hundreds of creatures which cause venomous bites. In America, there are relatively few venomous creatures which commonly attack humans. These creatures include bees, black widow spiders, brown recluse spiders, scorpions, gila monsters, and snakes. While bites by the majority of these creatures are uncommon in America, certainly, oil of oregano would be an absolutely necessary prescription for those exploring rain forests—as well as the wanderer/explorer in America's deserts.

The bee sting is the most commonly occurring venomous bite in America, and this kind of sting often results in serious allergic reactions. In fact, hundreds of deaths occur in America every year from bee stings, a dilemma that has become of tantamount importance since the advent of the Africanized killer bee.

Arriving from Mexico in the early 1990s the killer bee began invading the southern part of America, including Texas, New Mexico, Arizona, and Louisiana. It is a mutant bee made when geneticists crossed a type of African bee with a Western bee. It was a case of genetic meddling with the unpredictable powers of nature. The intention was to produce a more disease resistant honey bee, but the experiment turned sour. Instead, what developed was a bizarre type of swarming bee, which produced no honey. In fact, this aggressive Africanized bee began crowding out the good honey producing bees, fully displacing them from their territories. This bee is fickle; when provoked it may aggressively attack both animals and humans. Injecting its venom, it severely disables its victim and may cause death. In fact, several deaths in the Southwestern states have been linked to the Africanized bee. Oil of oregano will save lives in the event of bee stings, because it is an antivenom. This means it neutralizes venom on contact. However, it is highly versatile, meaning that it appears to neutralize the poisons of virtually any venomous creature. If a bite of any type occurs, medical attention must be sought immediately. However, the application of oil of oregano can only act as an aid if not an outright cure and certainly will do no harm.

Treatment protocol

If a venomous bite occurs, seek medical attention immediately. Apply oil of oregano liberally to the involved site. Repeat application every hour or as often as is necessary until improvement is noted. Then, apply three to four times daily until the wound heals completely. Take the oil sublingually, 2 or more drops as often as needed. Bee venom is minor issue to the powers of oil of oregano, which is capable of neutralizing even poison hemlock.

Vitiligo

This is defined as the loss of skin pigment. The skin normally contains cells, known as melanocytes, which produce pigment. If the cells become diseased, they fail to produce pigment, and white spots develop. It was recently discovered that fungi are the primary cause of vitiligo. The fungi apparently infect the melanocytes. These fungi actually feed off of these cells, destroying them. For the condition to be resolved the fungi must be destroyed.

Treatment protocol

Rub the oil of oregano on the skin, ideally using the SuperStrength variety. Also, take the oil internally, two or more drops under the tongue twice daily. Take also Oreganol gelcaps, one capsule twice daily. As an additional topical rub apply Skin Clenz crude essential oil formula. This formula contains a number of skin-nourishing and cleansing essential oils, including oils of bay leaf, lavender, borage, oregano, and more. Ideally, rub it on the skin after a hot shower. Apply the Skin Clenz at least once daily. To order Skin Clenz call: 1-800-243-5242.

Warts

Warts are among the most feared and despised of all infections, mainly because they are so ugly. However, they are also highly contagious.

Warts are caused by viral infection, the organism being known as a *papillomavirus*. The lesion it causes is appropriately known as a papilloma, which is essentially a tiny tumor, that is wart, of the skin cells. This tumor is the result of the ability of the wart virus to damage or control the genetics of the skin cells.

Oil of oregano contains a variety of antiviral compounds, although testing against the wart virus is limited. However, the oil will readily penetrate warts all the way to the root, and this will aid in their destruction and/or removal. Furthermore, the oil exhibits direct antiviral activities, plus it aids the immune system in destroying the virus. Clinical results are encouraging; one patient noted complete eradication of warts occurring upon the hands and soles of the feet after two months of treatment. If undergoing surgical or chemical removal, be sure to apply the oil to the wart site both prior to and after the surgery.

Treatment protocol

Apply the oil of oregano via a saturated cotton pad; hold the pad against the wart as long as possible. Repeat several times daily. Take several drops in juice, milk, or water twice daily. For tougher cases use the SuperStrength oil of wild oregano, topically as well as internally; take 5 to 20 drops twice daily under the tongue or in juice/water.

Wounds

Open wounds are certainly the most common injury occurring at home or work. In a large family it seems that almost every week someone is injured, especially if small children are around. It is hoped that if an injury is severe, the family doctor or, these days, the emergency room physician, can quickly solve the problem. However, what about the minor wounds that occur everyday? We lack that universal potion, that versatile cure-all that heals wounds and prevents catastrophes.

Oil of oregano is precisely that medicine chest in a bottle that we all desire and is the perfect treatment for any type of open wound. In terms of antiseptics the family medicine chest typically contains such things as hydrogen peroxide, mercurochrome, iodine, hexachlorophene (a chlorine-based antiseptic), and rubbing alcohol. Regarding the mercury-based mercurochrome, it is interesting to note that Taber's medical dictionary states that "its effectiveness is doubtful." Furthermore, Taber's notes that alcohol, iodine, and hexachlorophene, while capable of killing microbes, fail to kill the spores from which microbes germinate.

Oil of oregano supersedes all other over-the-counter antiseptics and, essentially, is superior to all commercial antiseptics combined. For instance, while iodine, hexachlorophene, and hydrogen peroxide can kill microbes, all have been found in scientific studies to also kill human cells. Furthermore, hydrogen peroxide causes extensive tissue damage and, thus, interferes with wound healing. Also, scientific studies show how hydrogen peroxide and hexachlorophene are carcinogenic when applied directly to open wounds. Iodine is less toxic to human tissues than hydrogen peroxide, but it is highly toxic if ingested, a toxicity which is exemplified by the labeling of the bottle with the familiar skull and crossbones. In contrast, oil of oregano destroys germs as well as their spores without damaging human tissues.

Open wounds are a cause for great anxiety, because there is always a risk of infection. The infection might be localized, but it may also become disseminated, that is it could reach the blood and/or internal organs. This is known commonly as blood poisoning, the medical term being sepsis. Necrotizing fasciitis, popularly known as flesh eating bacteria, is one form of this poisoning. Caused by bacteria, usually strep or staph, this infection is associated with massive tissue destruction occurring in various regions of the body. Usually, the infection originates when an open wound becomes contaminated with the causative bacteria. For whatever reason the immune system fails to contain the microbe, and it invades the body aggressively. While invading, these highly toxic microbes cause extensive destruction of the tissues, and no tissue is immune to their aggression. The microbes destroy tissues by secreting potent enzymes, which digest the tissues. Flesh eating bacteria is no contest for oil of oregano. Research proves that the bacteria which typically cause this disease, staph and strep, are decimated by the oil. The prompt use of this oil externally and internally entirely prevents the onset of this horrific infection.

Treatment protocol

Apply oil of oregano in the wound and along the wound edges: cover, if possible. Repeat application once or twice daily. For puncture wounds saturate the wound with oil of oregano; seek medical attention. For tougher cases use the SuperStrength oil of wild oregano, and apply liberally as needed. If irritation or pain occurs, discontinue use. To aid in healing take Oregamax capsules, three caps twice daily.

Chapter Three **Everyday Uses**

There are hundreds of practical uses for oil of oregano. In fact, its versatility for everyday needs seems infinite. About the time that all of its uses appear to have been discovered, yet another application is derived.

Microbes cause problems both in the home and in our bodies. Oil of oregano offers the benefit of "microbial control" for the home and the human body without the toxicity of chemical antiseptics. In contrast to commercially available antiseptics, such as hexachlorophene, chlorine, and betadine, oil of oregano won't damage home or body, because it is entirely non-toxic. Even the fumes of some of these commercially available substances are deadly, whereas the fumes of oil of oregano are healthy.

One reason oil of oregano is so valuable is because it is both an antiseptic and solvent, and this solvent action aids in the delivery of its useful attributes. This gives it great utility when added to cleaning solutions.

There are infinite uses for oil of oregano in everyday life. Certainly, new applications will be uncovered continuously. Let's review some of the everyday uses for oil of oregano and oregano spice.

In the Food

Oil of oregano is not a salad oil, but it has extensive applications in food preparation. Its primary utility is a result of its antimicrobial powers.

Use the oil and/or spice to prevent microbial growth in prepared foods. Add a drop or two of the oil in any picnic salad, especially those containing milk, meat, or eggs. Or, mix into the food a few capsules of Oregamax. This will greatly halt the growth of microbes and, thus, reduce the risk for food poisoning.

The role of fresh produce in the transmission of infection has become evident, because a variety of outbreaks of infection have been directly traced to specific fruits and/or vegetables. For instance, in 1996 a massive outbreak of E. coli infection in Illinois was traced to contaminated red leaf lettuce; hundreds were afflicted and over 30 individuals died. Alfalfa sprouts have caused the outbreak of both salmonella and E. coli. Also in 1996 a nation-wide outbreak of a parasitic infection known as Cyclospora occurred. Eventually, the source was traced to contaminated fruit, notably raspberries imported from Ecuador. In all likelihood they were served without being washed. The key word is "wash," because only a thorough washing/rinsing of the produce will offer protection; a cursory rinsing will probably fail to remove sufficient numbers of the organisms to obviate infection. When in doubt be sure to add a drop or two of oil of oregano in any fruit dish/vegetable dish.

It is important to realize that vegetables are just as likely to transmit microbial infections as are animal foods. For instance, in October 1996 the *Medical Tribune* reported that dozens of individuals in the United States suffered serious food poisoning from eating the classical vegetarian foods: iceberg lettuce and alfalfa sprouts. These vegetables were contaminated with salmonella and/or E. coli, both of which can cause life-threatening dysentery. The major outbreak occurred in Montana (1995) in which 70 people were affected. This outbreak pales in comparison to the one which occurred in April, 2000, in Walkerton, Ontario, Canada. As many as 3,000 people, virtually the entire population, were contaminated by a toxic form of E. coli known as E. Coli 01567:H7. This is a mutant form of E. Coli found in contaminated sausage or food. The medical system was overloaded: people were sent home to fend for themselves. Several people died. Many people have yet to recover from their symptoms. Interestingly, a few families used the Oreganol with stupendous results, one woman claiming it saved the life of her child.

When dining in restaurants the potential always exists for the contraction of infection, because there is no guarantee that the food is thoroughly washed. The rule is that salad vegetables in restaurants are frequently served without being washed. When in doubt take oil of oregano for protection, two or three drops in a glass of water or juice with meals.

No one can be sure where commercial produce comes from or how it is grown or handled. That is why it is a must to use oil of oregano as an insurance plan. After washing the produce thoroughly, soak it for a few moments in enough water to cover along with a couple of drops of oil of oregano. In particular, be sure to soak all commercial berries and leafy vegetables in an oil of oregano solution, as these are readily contaminated by microbes.

Oil of oregano, as well as the crushed herb, is safe for use in food. It makes an excellent condiment added to soup, sauces, entrees, and salads. Use them freely in any food or recipe.

A Sterile Kitchen?

While the kitchen is certainly not a desirable place for microbes to grow, they do so freely. Wherever food is prepared, it becomes a breeding ground for their prolific growth, especially if the area isn't cleaned properly. Yet, the rule is wherever food exists is where microbes reside no matter how "squeaky clean" it appears.

While a clean appearing kitchen is desirable, all of the scrubbing in the world is no guarantee that it is microscopically clean. However, by using oil of oregano a sort of sterility can be achieved. Since the kitchen houses our food, it is crucial to keep it as clean microbially as possible. Oil of oregano is a godsend for this purpose. Simply use a small amount, like five or ten drops for every pint, in cleaning solutions in order to gain that antiseptic effect. Clean counter tops, sinks, stoves, and refrigerators with a cleaning solution containing the oil. Add a few drops in the dish water. Keep the dish rag or sponge sterile by adding a few drops after usage. The latter are readily contaminated by microbes.

Why use it instead of commercial cleaner? The reason is oil of oregano and its fumes are non-toxic. When used in a mild soap solution, it is equally as effective as commercial cleaners, and it is safe to use around food.

A special type of cleaning oregano is now available. It is for use anywhere in the house. It can also be used to cleanse vegetables/fruit of germs and other contaminants. Add it to dish soap, or put a few drops on the dish sponge to prevent germs from growing. Also, use it to clean the refrigerator: a natural residue remains, keeping germs from growing. It is perfect for adding in dishwashers during the washing cycle as well as in the washing machine. Oregano oil has solvent properties, so it greatly aids in the removal of dirt as well as stains. Called Cleaning Oregano, it may be ordered by calling 1-800-243-5242.

Microbes in the Air, Anyone?

It is difficult to imagine that disease travels through the air we breath. Indeed, microbes abound in the air and are even found circulating in the most inhospitable climates from mountain tops to the North and South Poles.

Microbes are found in the greatest numbers in the air of inhabited regions, especially indoors. The home is laced with microbes of all varieties, and the greatest numbers are found in the kitchen and bathroom. Public restrooms are particularly notorious for harboring airborne germs, as are public eating facilities. Most of us just don't realize that the air in our homes and work environments contains billions of microbes in the form of yeasts, molds, bacteria, and viruses. However, perhaps the worst place for these germs is at work in closed buildings. Essentially, the germs have no where to go but into a host, depositing themselves on human skin as well as within the body, like in the lungs, sinuses, or digestive tract.

Oil of oregano is one of the most volatile of all essential oils. This means that it readily vaporizes into the air. This property makes it ideal for sterilizing air. Mix a few drops of oregano oil in water in a spray bottle and mist the entire house. The energy in the air will change immediately. The bacteria, mold, and virus counts will be significantly reduced. As a result you will feel the difference.

Keeping the Kids In Line

Children are major victims of infectious disease, plus they spread it readily. Children usually fail to carefully attend to hygiene. Their hand washing technique is usually poor, if they wash at all.

Oil of oregano makes life easier and safer in the home, especially if children are around. Simply add it to all pump soaps. Instruct children to wash their hands with the soap after using the restroom. Train them to wash their hands thoroughly. Be sure they also wash their hands after eating, as food residue on the hands feeds microbial growth.

The fingernails are one of the dirtiest regions of children, microbially. The undersides of the nails often contain a reservoir of microbes, especially if the nails are long. It is well known that parasitic infections in children are spread by poor hygiene; an entire day care center can become infected from one carrier. The hands are the main mode of transmission, but it is the undersides of the fingernails that house the parasitic cysts and eggs. Physicians know that children cannot be cured of pinworm infection, unless their hands and nails are kept clean, because, otherwise, children continuously re-infect themselves. The eggs of the pinworms become lodged under the nails when children scratch their buttocks. Oil of oregano destroys the eggs and helps keep the hands sterile.

A Sterile Bathroom?

The bathroom is a hotbed for microbial overgrowth. Here, they are found everywhere and in incredibly large amounts. Microbiologists know that if they want to grow the greatest number and variety of microbes possible, all they need to do is set up their experiments in a restroom. The fact that any bathroom or restroom contains billions of microbes is one thing you can count on. Obviously, reducing the microbe count in the restroom is a necessary goal. However, why do this with caustic chemicals, which may be more injurious than the microbes themselves? Instead, use oil of oregano as a cleaning solution. It can be safely mixed with any soap-based cleaner. Put a few drops in the toilet bowl every day. Be sure to keep bath sponges "oregano oiled."

Toothbrushes are a breeding ground for microbes. Tests show that the average toothbrush is teeming with microbes, many of which arise from the restroom air. Be sure to soak the toothbrush in a solution of oil of oregano, salt, and water. Ideally, keep the brush and soak outside the restroom, and bring it in only when using it. Add a couple of drops of oil of oregano to the toothbrush; use as a dentrifice. The oil dramatically reduces plaque formation. Often, there is no need for toothpaste, which saves money, plus toothpastes often contain noxious substances, like food dyes and fluoride. There is no need for fluoride when using oil of oregano. It destroys germs, strengthens the gums, and tightens the teeth. What a tremendous benefit from a natural non-toxic substance. Germs destroy the dental tissues and lead to tooth and gum disease. If the germs are destroyed, the dental system remains healthy. This is precisely what the Oreganol accomplishes. Also, the teeth need minerals. Oregamax provides microdoses of crude calcium, magnesium, and phosphorus, naturally strengthening the teeth; take 2 or 3 capsules twice daily.

Chapter Four   **Oregano to the Rescue**

Since ancient times oregano has been used to benefit humanity. The first recorded use was by the Assyrians in 3,000 B.C; who described numerous medicinal applications. For centuries the Greeks made extensive use of it, as did the Romans. It is a Biblical medicine, and few people realize that wild Mediterranean oregano is the original Bible hyssop. This implies that it may have been used since the time of Abraham or perhaps earlier.

The word for oregano in the ancient Bible is ezov, which is Hebrew. This word was mistranslated by the English as hyssop. This leads to confusion, because the herb hyssop is completely different botanically than wild oregano. It was Dr. Fleisher of New York who finally made the distinction. Taking his team to the Sinai, he scaled the mountains. Growing everywhere, he found wild oregano, but no hyssop. Thus, it appears certain that wild oregano is the "purifying herb" so highly distinguished in the Bible. Mamonidies, Jewish scholar and famous naturalistic physician of Islamic Spain, clearly stated that the so-called hyssop of the Law is simply the wild oregano of the Mediterranean mountains.

Despite oregano's wondrous ancient history the Western world has never availed itself of its immense benefits, that is until recently. Of all of the trade journals searched in the preparation of this book, that is the magazines that you can buy in the marketplace, only one was on oregano. As a result, the American and Canadian public suffer an information void about this invaluable substance.

The ancients certainly used oregano as a seasoning, and it still is used as such. The difference is they also used it as a medicine, because their experience proved that its regular use helped ward off infection and disease. All parts of the plant were utilized, including the fresh herb, dried crumbled leaves, and root. The forms in which it was administered included the essential oil, hot infusions made from the leaves/roots, and the crushed fresh herb as a poultice. All of these uses are valuable, and it is likely that a combination of these forms will elucidate the greatest benefits, since a large intake may be required, especially in the treatment of stubborn diseases.

As a food oregano is highly versatile. It is often combined with other herbs, vegetables, or oils which enhance or potentiate not only its flavor but also its chemical composition and immune enhancing properties. Oregano blends well with fats and is especially versatile when used with red meats, poultry, fatty fish, cheese, and extra virgin olive oil. Spices which compliment or enhance its richness include garlic, onion, mint, sage, sour grape, and *Rhus coriaria* (mountain sumac). Interestingly, the latter grows in concert with oregano and is found as the second ingredient in Oregamax. Rhus coriaria is a nutritionally rich and sour tasting herb which is an excellent condiment for meat dishes. It is the top naturally occurring source of malic, gallic, and tannic acids, themselves natural antiseptics. A recent study documents that Rhus coriaria possesses significant anti-viral actions. It is also an excellent source of naturally occurring vitamin C. Since oregano is devoid of vitamin C, Rhus coriaria compliments it superbly, which illustrates the wisdom of a botanical formula such as Oregamax, which contains both wild oregano and wild Rhus.

The best oregano spice should be a medium green color. It can be turned into a rich or bright green by heating or by cooking it in oil. Most of the supermarket or health food store sources of the dried herb are a dull, lifeless, drab olive color, and this is undesirable. Standardization is also undesirable, because this connotes a chemical treatment. Herbs are delicate. They shouldn't be treated with harsh chemicals such as solvents or even alcohol. Beware of poor quality and/or standardized types of wild oregano supplements. Select only the crude unprocessed types of wild oregano, the type used in antiquity and the type referenced in the holy texts. The North American Herb and Spice Company, 1-800-243-5242, offers fresh premium grade wild oregano products and nutritional supplements. These products are 100% wild and are never standardized or treated with chemicals.

Hippocrates said that food is the best medicine. However, the FDA mandates that food or herbs absolutely do not cure. Fortunately, we are still able to make our own decisions and choices in this realm.

What the ancients did is one thing, but the utility oregano offers today is what is critical. People living in modern civilizations are extensively victimized by infectious disease. Medicine offers little if any hope for curing these infections. Everyone is at risk for attack. This vulnerability is a consequence of the extremely potent and widespread germs which are a creation of modern life. It is the result of drug-resistant germs, viral epidemics, parasites/bacteria in the water, bizarre pathogenic yeasts and fungi, the intake of immunosuppressive drugs, hospital supergerms, excessive antibiotic intake, and genetically engineered mutants. It is also the result of the fact that our immune systems are weakened from poor nutrition, stress, and/or drugs. In other words, the risks are higher than ever before in today's civilization, because the individual might be healthy–never sick a day in his/her life–and still succumb to a bizarre infection.

This is where wild oregano, the "hyssop of the Law", comes to the rescue. This is the most potent health-inducing herb known. The best way to prove this is to test the herb on human beings. The following case histories were reported by individuals who used oregano to alleviate health problems and in some cases even to reverse life-threatening incidents. They represent unbiased reports and give an accurate representation of the immense value which oregano spice and oil have as natural medicines.

Family flu cured in three days: Mr. and Mrs. M., both in their later seventies, had the flu with all of the typical irritating and debilitating symptoms such as severe weakness, coughing, aching, and congestion. For almost six weeks neither could make significant progress. Both began taking an oregano supplement, Oregamax, along with two drops of the unrefined oil 3 times daily. Within three days the unremitting symptoms had disappeared and the infection was eliminated.

Root canal aborted: An optometrist, Dr. P., was plagued with an abscessed tooth. He was scheduled for a root canal and did not want to take antibiotics. As suggested he put a few drops of Oreganol™ oil of oregano (a combination of oil of oregano and a fine grade of extra virgin olive oil) on a small piece of sterile cotton and placed it between the cheek and the infected tooth, changing it twice daily. Within three days the swelling and infection were entirely eradicated.

Hearing loss abated: Dr. R., a nutritionally-oriented chiropractor, has helped countless patients get well, but he couldn't seem to get his family to listen to his advice. Thus, he watched with horror while his brother-in-law lost much of his hearing due to chronic infections. Finally, when the brother-in-law realized that the medical treatment had failed, he appealed for help. Dr. R. determined that his new patient had a 40% hearing loss due to an infection in the middle ear. After using a diluted drop of oil of oregano in each ear on a daily basis for a week, the infection and also the hearing impairment were entirely eliminated.

Dangerous spider bite cured: Mrs. D. lives in a lovely antebellum mansion with many nooks and crannies. It is a haven for brown recluse spiders. One night as she was preparing for her evening shower Mrs. D. noticed a red bite on the right side of her rib cage. She thought it must be a mosquito bite, applied some tea tree oil, and retired for the night. By morning she was intensely ill, her face and torso were red and swollen; the bite had become an inflamed mass about 4 inches in diameter. She was evaluated at the emergency room, but there seemed to be no treatment available. Soon after returning home the center of the bite began to show the signs of necrosis, as is classical for brown recluse bites. Her sister, familiar with the antivenom properties of oil of oregano, drove several hundred miles with a supply of the oil. By the time she arrived the victim appeared to be in shock and was extremely weak. The oil was generously applied to the lesion, and it was also taken internally. To keep it from evaporating the wound was covered with raw honey and Telfa pads. Along with the topical treatment she took Oregamax, six capsules four times daily and 3 drops of the oil by mouth 4 times daily. Within seventy-two hours the tissue destruction was eliminated, and the violent flu-like symptoms, redness, weakness, and swelling were gone. Thus, incredibly, the potentially disfiguring spider bite was entirely resolved.

Poison ivy defeated quickly: Mrs. J. maintains a beautiful yard and garden; she considers working in this capacity to be therapeutic. However, every year she is a victim of poison ivy. Her sensitivity is so acute that she breaks out in a rash no matter how carefully she avoids contact with it. With her last outbreak, she applied the oil of oregano to the rash. Immediate relief of the itching was noted. Within four days the rash and weeping sores were entirely healed.

Massive sunburn halted: Ms. K., a fair skinned lady, was visiting friends in the Carribean. Her friends were sea shell hounds, and a recent hurricane left the beaches littered with them. They spent the whole morning admiring and picking up the shells, but by noon Ms. G. was severely sunburned. She couldn't even walk without severe pain. In excruciating pain she made it home, and applied the oil of oregano on the burned skin. What should have become a severe blistering burn never blistered. There was not even any peeling, and incredibly, the pain was eliminated within 24 hours.

No bruising when there should have been: Mrs. J. enjoyed playing with her very active and delightful pet kitten. However, in a short time the raw meat-fed energetic kitten became a strong, muscular cat, and he remained playful. One evening she interrupted her work to play with the cat vigorously. After an extended play period, she returned to work. She grabbed her laptop computer and began walking away. Still in the play mode her cat tackled her in mid stride. Mrs. G. hit the concrete floor with both knees and then both elbows. The pain was so intense that it first seemed that knees and elbows must be broken. A doctor friend came by and ruled out fracture. Oil of oregano was applied immediately to the injured area which helped eliminate the pain. Even more astounding was the fact no bruising occurred where the oil was applied. With an injury of this extent severe bruising and swelling would be expected, and Mrs. G. tends to bruise easily. Mrs. G. continued to apply the oil and was able to walk unassisted within twenty-four hours.

Chronic spinal pain relieved: Mr. C. suffered from chronic stiffness, pressure, and pain in his upper back over the spine. This developed after a prolonged illness, which left him unable to function. The pain in the upper thoracic spine was unremitting, but he also complained of sudden episodes of muscle contractions in the upper back, stating that his spine "locked up." He had tried various rubs and oils, but nothing seemed to work. Oil of oregano was applied twice daily. He also consumed 12 capsules daily of Oregamax. Pain relief was almost immediate, and he noticed a great improvement that lasted for several days. This was the first treatment which had ever produced prolonged relief. His improvement was so great that he is now able to assume a full work load for the first time in six years.

Pus comes out by the cup: Mr. S. suffered for several years from poor health. His illness developed after a severe case of diarrhea. Suddenly, he noticed a small hole (fistula) on his left knee. Occasionally, a small amount of pus-like material could be extruded. For several years it would open and drain a pussy substance and then seem to disappear. Finally, it became overtly inflamed due to a rather severe blow. Antibiotics failed to eradicate the problem, and parasitic infection of the knee was suspected. The swelling and infection became so severe that blood poisoning seemed imminent. Mr. S.'s therapy consisted of applying oil of oregano combined with hot packs. In addition, he took large amounts of Oregamax by mouth. In four days the swelling, which was a massive five inches in diameter, was decreased to about a two inch wound. Then, the knee exuded copious amounts of pus and bloody fluid, nearly one cup in all. After suffering with this condition for almost six years, the infection in the knee was eradicated within two weeks due to conscientious treatment with the hot packs and oil of oregano.

Big man brought back on his feet: Along with festivities and a sharing of gifts and cheer, Chistmas Day also is a prime time to pass along cold and flu bugs. Christmas Day almost the entire L. family suffered from a particularly vicious strain of flu which seemed to last for around ten days to several weeks. John, a big sturdy fellow, took great pride in the fact that he rarely succumbed to viruses like the rest of the family did and was very vocal about it. However, on Christmas day he not only fell prey to the flu bug, but he also was so ill he couldn't conduct the traditional family activities. He finally forced himself out of bed to join in opening gifts, but the big man was steadily sliding down in his huge overstuffed chair. A family member unable to stand by and watch this miserable mass of humanity suffer further gave him six Oregamax along with a glass of water spiked with three drops of oil of oregano. His wife watched him carefully, since he had always adamantly refused to take nutritional supplements. Within 10 minutes he was up walking around and able to function. By the next day he was able to stay out of bed most of the day and was totally well the day after. The former Mr. Skeptical had second thoughts about using supplements and now readily takes them. What a great Christmas present that was.

Small boy's bronchial infection halted: Alex, an active three year old, suffered from frequent bronchial infections and had an almost continuous deep racking cough. His mother constantly gave him an over-the-counter children's cough syrup which had virtually no impact on the hacking cough. As the cough became more croupy the child was given a small glass of water and one drop of oil of oregano. Almost immediately the cough loosened. Within thirty minutes the child was no longer coughing, and he remained free of the cough for the rest of the day.

Urinary infection eradicated: Mrs. S. was taking care of her aged mother, who had developed a severe kidney and bladder infection after taking a regimen of antibiotics for a different health problem. Although she was instructed to administer only two drops of oil of oregano daily, in her eagerness to help she gave her mother five drops. Interestingly, her mother improved within three hours after the first dose. Pain upon urination, urgency, and burning were all diminished and her urinary flow returned to normal. With continued treatment, the kidney/bladder infection was eradicated.

A new face and a new life: Mr. M. suffered from rosacea of the nasal region for twenty-five years. His nose always appeared red and inflamed. For years he tried an endless stream of hopeful cures, yet neither drugs nor nutritional remedies provided any relief. He was skeptical of trying another treatment but was reluctant to give up hope. Mr. M. took three Oregamax twice daily and used three drops of the Oreganol internally. He also applied the oil topically on a daily basis. After twenty-five days the periphery of the nose was a normal color and texture with only the center remaining discolored. His treatment is ongoing and a complete cure is anticipated.

10 years of irritable bowel improved dramatically: Ms. B., whose diet was admittedly poor, suffered from an "incurable" case of spastic colon and diarrhea. Even with healthy food, she did poorly, and whenever she ate, she made sure a restroom was near. If she went out to eat, she sat near the restroom. After only two weeks of taking the oil of oregano and Oregamax, the restroom dependency was eliminated: the spasms and diarrhea were halted, and her life returned to normal.

Emergency replacement surgery avoided: Mr. C. suffered from shoulder pain so severe that he finally consented to surgery. Just prior to his appointment at the hospital, he decided to apply the oil of oregano, hopeful that it might provide just enough relief to get a good night's sleep. Much to his surprise after a week of applying the oil the pain was gone, and he had freedom of movement in his shoulders. Mr. C. canceled his date with the surgeon and saved himself a lot of money and needless agony.

Potential fungal invasion halted: Mrs. K. attended a business meeting in a warm climate at a large resort area. She was always fastidious about her personal cleanliness and was horrified when she developed what seemed to be an extremely sore cut on the underside of the small toe. It refused to heal, and the doctor diagnosed it as athlete's foot which was likely contracted at the hotel. Within three days of applying the oil of oregano the soreness was gone and the open sore was mostly healed. Regular application has entirely prevented any recurrence.

Genital Herpes Disappears: Rusty is a very self-protective lady, who is highly in tune with her body; she knows when something works. Suffering from genital herpes for several years, she had given up hope until finding the wild oregano. An outbreak in the buttocks was incredibly painful. She applied the oregano oil, which halted the pain. She took the Oreganol and Oregamax internally and within a month she experienced a complete eradication of the problem, never to return.

Splinter extruded with ease: Donna restores antiques for her home and for occasional resale. While stripping an old chest of drawers, a tiny splinter became lodged in her finger. It was too small to grasp with tweezers, yet it was amazingly painful. After two days the area became red and irritated. Fearing infection she applied a drop of oregano oil, and the pain was immediately diminished. By the next day the oregano oil caused the splinter to surface, and it was easily removed. The soreness and inflammation were also eliminated.

Unrelenting stomachache resolved: Mr. T. is an avid outdoorsman who enjoys camping and exploring. While trekking through the bush he found a fresh water spring bubbling up through a crack in the rocks. His thirst was profound, and the water was clear, sweet, and inviting. It just didn't seem possible that it could be contaminated. However, within twenty-four hours after drinking the spring water, it became violently apparent that something was wrong. He suffered from all of the debilitating symptoms of waterborne parasitic infection. Even after treatment for parasitic infestation Mr. T. experienced chronic stomach pain, which was especially evident upon awakening. Parasites become more active when a food source is not available, and this explains the increased sensitivity in the morning. His nutritionist suggested that he take oil of oregano each day. After four days the stomach pain, which he suffered with daily for over five years, was eradicated.

Warts disappear; fungal infection cured: Ms. C. suffered from a litany of infections for several years, and no one was able to help her. For over five years she tried every type of conventional and alternative medicine to no avail. Literally hundreds of herbal and vitamin supplements failed her. As the area in which she lived was a repository of alternative medicine, she had been treated by a plethora of naturally inclined practitioners. Medical doctors were also seen, and, while they were confounded, they did diagnose a fungal infection. She was placed on antifungal drugs, which gave her a modicum of relief. Despite previous treatment she had warts on her hands and soles of her feet, viral infection in her lungs, and fungal infestation on her hands. She also suffered from chronic fatigue, itchy skin, chronic allergies, and heavy plaque on the teeth. The fatigue had been attributed to a chronic systemic viral infection.

Fortunately, Ms. C. procured oil of oregano and decided to administer a large dosage: 10 drops three times daily. To take this amount she placed the drops in gelatin capsules. Within just a few weeks, her warts were entirely cleared, the hand fungus was absolved, the fatigue was virtually eliminated, and the systemic viral infection improved significantly. For the first time in five years she was able to stop taking antifungal drugs. Interestingly, although the oil was only taken internally, she noticed a significant reduction in plaque formation in the mouth, indicating a generalized antiseptic action within the body. These improvements are medically impressive if not clearly miraculous.

Coach cured of Irishman's disease: Coach J., a 61 year old male, contacted me to let me know that his Irish stubbornness (I would call it toughness) eventually paid off. He decided to buy oil of oregano for what he thought was a "strange use": alcoholic neuritis. It turns out that the coach was formerly a heavy drinker, who was left with alcohol-induced nerve damage. His symptoms included pain and numbness in his calf muscles. While all other medical treatments had failed, incredibly, after regular application of oil of oregano the symptoms dramatically improved and the neuritis virtually disappeared.

Almost quit, but saved by the bell: Mrs. B. is a feisty 60 year old, who wouldn't give up on curing her problem: suffocation and severe sinus infection, as well as sinus headaches. She frequently couldn't breath. When doctors put her on a harsh medicine, the side effects were so extreme that she couldn't sit still, in other words, the drug made her agitated. When she complained to the doctors, they brazenly told her, "either learn to sit still, or suffocate." This sent Mrs. B. on a mission: she ordered the oreganol and took it at night. However, she felt a bit choked after taking it and despised the taste. She thought, "This isn't for me, so I will send it back." However, miraculously, by the next morning her breathing improved dramatically and her excruciatingly painful sinus headache was gone. She now keeps at least a dozen bottles of the oil handy and claims, *"I'll never live without it."*

Scalp condition improves immediately: Don, a busy executive, had a severe case of seborrhea of the scalp. It was itchy, unsightly, and frustratingly resistant to treatment. Hair loss seemed to be associated with the condition. Don was instructed to apply several drops of oil of oregano to his scalp after washing his hair. A reduction in the itching was noticed immediately. Within two weeks the embarrassing highly visible scaling was significantly reduced.

Tooth and gum infection quickly cured: Mr. K., a 40-year-old male, still had his wisdom teeth and felt fortunate, until he developed an infection. His left wisdom tooth was aching and the gums surrounding it were swollen and extremely painful. He couldn't chew on that side of the mouth without extreme pain. Mr. K. was instructed to apply the oil of oregano directly on top of the tooth and to vigorously rub it on the gum tissue surrounding the tooth. Within three days significant relief of the pain and swelling was noted. After five days of treatment the infection was eliminated, and he was able to again chew without pain.

Sinus pain and congestion disappears: Mrs. J., a 42-year-old woman, suffered from chronic sinus congestion and sinus headaches for 15 years. She had seen numerous doctors and tried dozens of medications to no avail. Her main complaint was miserable sinus headaches that no amount of aspirin or Acetaminophen could relieve. It was to the point where she hated to awaken in the morning, because she routinely suffered from congestion and post nasal drip. Mrs. J. took one capsule of Oregamax (which contains wild oregano, Rhus coriaria, garlic, and onion) twice daily. Within a week she improved dramatically; whenever she takes the Oregamax her sinuses drain and the headaches are relieved. Incredibly, for the first time in 15 years she is free of sinus pressure and headaches—as long as she continues to take the Oregamax.

Serious hospital-acquired infection aborted: An eighty-one year old woman was in the hospital for three weeks due to sudden and unexplained seizures. Her temperature was elevated intermittently, usually at night. After extensive testing the doctors were unable to determine the cause of her condition. She was placed in a nursing home to continue her convalescence. Within two days she developed a constant cough, back pain, and was unable to eat. Her lungs were filling with fluid, she could not sit up for any length of time, and she was a pale, pasty color. She was given two drops of oil of oregano in water. Almost immediately her cough diminished, and by evening she was able to sit up without discomfort. By morning her color had improved, the cough had disappeared, her appetite had returned, and there were no further signs of a lung infection.

A 20 year case of bronchitis resolved: Mrs. S. called to report that her husband was delighted with the results of taking oil of oregano. He had suffered all of the aggravating symptoms of bacterial bronchitis for over twenty years. In just one week of taking oil of oregano his condition was vastly improved.

Allergic cough halted immediately: Mrs. R. had a history of seasonal allergies, which reliably resurfaced every year. The allergies were so bothersome that she regularly underwent allergy injections. She suffered a relapse during the fall; an unusual amount of rainfall heightened her mold allergies. As usual, she developed post nasal drip and cough during the outbreak. A friend brought over a bottle of Oreganol™ and gave her a mere drop in a glass of water. Within minutes she felt relief and her allergic misery and the cough, which was previously unrelenting, disappeared.

Severe Night Cramps Eliminated: Mr. B. is a stocky no-nonsense individual who often takes advantage of his strong constitution by eating poorly. Apparently, after a late night sugary snack he developed severe foot cramps. Remembering that Oregamax is an excellent source of crude calcium and magnesium he took 4 capsules. Within minutes the foot cramps were halted. Note: this illustrates the value of crude unprocessed herbs as a source of minerals. In other words, the types of minerals contained in these herbs, while rather low in milligrams compared to synthetic mineral tablets, are well tolerated and absorbed. Oregamax may be taken as a crude natural calcium/magnesium supplement, 6 to 8 capsules daily.

Almost missed his TV appearance: Mr. A. was scheduled to appear on a national TV show promoting his new book. However, he was certain he would have to cancel because of a bad case of allergic rhinitis. Put simply, his nose wouldn't stop running, nor could he stop sneezing. He wondered if he could wipe his nose between camera shots, but the fact is he was truly in a bind. Per my instructions (and this should only be done under doctors orders) Mr. A. placed a drop of the oil directly into the nostril on each side. Within seconds he noticed relief; the sneezing halted and the dripping was lessened. After eating, the symptoms were reactivated but were not as severe. He administered another drop in each nostril. The results were spectacular; the unrelenting runny nose was stopped completely and the sneezing fits were halted. As a result, his TV appearance was a success.

Skin cancer "erased": Ms. S., a health food store owner in southern Florida, had a previous history of skin cancer, which developed on her forehead. It recurred and began growing rapidly. She applied the oil of oregano directly on the cancer several times daily. Within a week the cancer was completely eradicated.

Saved from Near Fatal Spinal Infection: Ms. S. had reason to be concerned: she had contracted Cryptococcus neoformans, a fungal infection of the spinal cord, which is routinely fatal. The fungus had infected her entire spinal column as well as the brain. A type of fungal meningitis, it is regarded as incurable. Drugs completely failed, even though she received them directly through a surgical opening in the spine. Ms. S. heard about the Oreganol and Oregamax on the radio. Taking no chances she bought the SuperStrength variety, and rubbed it on the spine around her shunt. She took the Oregamax and SuperStrength internally. After two weeks she went back to the hospital. Incredibly, she was culture negative, that is there was no sign of infection. Plus, the doctors asked, "What smells so good?--it is like pizza." However, Ms. S., unfortunately, was too afraid to tell them about her natural cure.

Chapter Five

The Hygiene Medicine

A recent survey published in USA Today illustrated how "unhygienic" the modern world is. The investigators found that fully 40% of all Americans, men and women, fail to wash their hands after using the restroom, that is public restrooms. Negligence of hygiene is a serious offense. This is because it is a certainty that a lack of cleanliness impairs health, both in the offender and in those with whom he/she is in contact.

Imagine the dastardly circumstance. The individual is hygienic and routinely washes the hands. Then, he/she grasps a railing or doornob just touched by a person who falters in hygiene, for instance, a person, who fails to wash their hands after answering the call of nature. The 'clean' person contracts, for instance, E. coli and becomes sickened, or even dies. Yet, this could happen to anyone, hygienic or unhygienic. No one is immune to the consequences of faulty hygiene.

Lack of careful attention to hygiene is a primary cause of the transmission of infections throughout the world, and America is no exception. Microbes are easily transmitted from direct contact with other humans as well as animals. Although this may surprise many individuals, microbial infections can also be readily contracted from inanimate objects.

The hands are an unsuspecting agent in the transmission of infections. For instance, an individual may have a cold; a sneeze is covered with the bare hand. Then, he/she shakes someone's hand. That person might use their newly contaminated hand to eat or might rub the face, eyes, or nose, leading to infection. Although most of us hate to think of it, as reiterated previously, a large percentage of people fail to wash their hands after urinating and/or defecating. Certainly, infection may be transmitted from these "unhygienic" individuals by hand shakes. However, imagine the potential dilemma that might occur if the contaminated individual is a food handler. Diaper changing is another means of fecal-oral contamination. Millions of diapers are changed every day. The potential for spread of disease is enormous, especially if there is failure to conduct careful hand washing. Many mothers may unthinkingly change the diapers and not even wash the hands, and this dangerous practice can cause infection in the mother as well as in uncountable other individuals.

In America we might take a greater number of showers than any other nation of the world, but there is widespread negligence in attention to careful hygiene, especially hand washing. No wonder contagious infections, such as hepatitis, meningitis, flu, colds, encephalitis, food poisoning, and giardiasis, remain endemic in America.

Oil of oregano helps reduce the risk for contracting microbial infections. It can be used both on the body and on inanimate objects. It may be added to soaps and body washes. It is a universal antiseptic, and there is no limit to the versatility of its uses. Let's review some of the potential uses of oil of oregano for daily hygiene.

Hand washing technique

Add oil of oregano to soap. Obviously, pump soaps are the ideal medium. They are also preferable because bar soaps tend to breed bacteria, especially if they are left in the open air in bathrooms. If bar soaps are used, add the oil directly to the bar before washing. Be sure to add it to soaps when washing in public restrooms. To wash hands, pump soap into the palm and turn on the water. Vigorously wash hands and rinse with copious amounts of water. Dry by using a fresh linen or paper towel. Use a paper towel to open the door, if using a public washroom. Touching the door handle will re-contaminate the hands, and this causes infection.

When traveling or out in public, there is another option: Germ-a-Clenz spray. This spice-oil based spray may be sprayed on the hands and used as a hand-cleanser. It is ideal to use when in public where water is not always available. Use it also to spray on the hands after hand-shaking. This will prevent the transmission of germs. A purse size of this spray is available.

Showering

Add a few drops of oil of oregano to liquid or bar soap, and wash the skin gently yet thoroughly. For washing hair add a few drops to shampoo. The oil helps eradicate scalp fungus as well as mites, the latter being a cause of baldness. It also conditions the hair, giving it strength and texture. Avoid contact with eyes.

There is another novel use for the oil: fume therapy. Simply rub a dropperful or so of the oil on the floor of a shower, where the water sprays. The heat from this spray volatilizes the oil, creating a titillating effect. Such an aromatherapy stimulates the senses, creating a kind of therapeutic shower. Or, mist the multiple spice spray in the shower, that is the Germ-a-Clenz.

The Feet

The feet may harbor a variety of microbes. In fact, they are one of the most commonly infected external sites on the body. Circulation in this area is poor, and this leads to sluggish local immunity. A variety of microbes may find residence in the skin of the feet, particularly between the toes, where moisture is retained. Foul odor is a dependable sign of poor health of the feet, as is the development of scaling or athlete's foot.

Toenails may readily become infected, particularly by fungi, although bacteria, such as Pseudomonas, may also infect them. Toenail infections are difficult to eradicate, because the infection begins deep within the nail bed, and the delivery of medicine to this region is difficult.

It is a little known fact that poor health of the feet affects the health of the entire body. Thus, for optimal health the feet must be kept clean and free of infection. Wash the feet often and be sure to keep the toenails well manicured. Clean any debris that might accumulate about the toenails or between the toes. Rub Oreganol once or twice daily over the nailbeds, the soles, and between the toes. Yet, for ideal results internal treatment is also required. Take the Oreganol under the tongue, 10 or more drops twice daily. Hold it under the tongue as long as possible. For optimal results it may take as long as six months of daily therapy, both topically and internally.

Don't neglect the health of the feet. The body will pay a price as a result.

Many people suffer from malodorous feet. This may be due to infection, including yeast infection. Regardless of the cause the oil is the answer. Simply rub on the feet in the morning and then apply over this the socks. Quickly, the foul odor is eliminated.

Dental health

The health of the teeth and gums affects every other tissue in the body. If the dental tissues are diseased, so will be the rest of the body. The connection is clear: if the individual neglects dental hygiene, he/she is neglecting overall health. Diseased gums and teeth have been clearly associated as a cause of heart disease, kidney disease, arthritis, liver disease, lung disease, and even cancer.

Oil of oregano keeps the entire dental system in optimal health. It reduces plaque and, in some instances, eliminates it. The oil strengthens the gums, reducing bleeding and pain. What's more, its solvent properties provide a cleansing action to remove stains, germs, and hardened plaque.

For foul breath the Oreganol is ideal. Simply rub on the gums morning and night or use on the toothbrush. Or, spray the mouth with Germ-a-Clenz, the natural water-soluble spice spray, which immediately eliminates any odor. This makes the ideal breath spray. Plus, it is chemical-free and, thus, is ideal for the chemically-sensitive.

Outdoors

When trekking in the wilderness the possibilities for a health disaster are endless. Furthermore, if an individual plans a prolonged wilderness trip, obviously, access to medical care is limited or perhaps nonexistent. Thus, it is important to maintain a readily available medicine kit.

Oil of oregano is the antiseptic of choice for the outdoor medical kit. Keep it in the back pack. If water is unavailable, use a small amount on hands after contact with germs. The Oreganol gelcaps are handy. They can't spill or break, since they are hermetically sealed and are contained in a compact plastic bottle. What's more, they are easily swallowed even without water. Wounds may occur in the outdoors where there is no clean water available. Add a few drops of oil of oregano on open wounds. Wash the wound as soon as water is available. If no water is available, oil of oregano is invaluable, whether for treating wounds or simply washing hands. It will keep the wound sterile until further treatment can be administered. It will also prevent the spread of infection until the hands can be properly washed.

Children

Be sure to educate children regarding the importance of hand washing. Oil of oregano should be part of every child's school locker. Infections spread like wildfires in public establishments, especially schools. Instruct children to use the oil during hand washing to prevent the transmission of infection from child to child and also to prevent it from arriving at the home. Fingernail health is often neglected in children. Dirty fingernails transmit infection, as microbes readily live under the nail bed. In particular, parasites tend to reside under the nails, and from there they are readily reintroduced into the body. The fingernails must be kept neatly trimmed. Wash the edges of the nail beds with a soap and oil of oregano solution. If this is done regularly, the incidence of infectious disease in children will be curbed dramatically.

The oil, that is the edible spice extract, can also be given to children internally. A drop or two daily will keep them in optimal health. In infants or newborns the spice oil is safe; beware of potentially toxic imitations. Use the Oreganol by rubbing it on the feet or chest as often as needed.

After Contact

Infections are readily spread after close contact among humans. Everyone is aware that infections may be spread from sexual intercourse, however, kissing, hugging, sneezing, and hand shaking may all disseminate infection. To avoid being a victim keep the oil of oregano handy at all times. Use it directly upon potentially contaminated skin; inhale it, rub it on the gums, and wash with it. Also, spray any potentially contaminated region with the Germ-a-Clenz, which is also ideal for spraying on clothing. Do whatever is necessary to avoid contracting a potentially unforgiving disease.

The Traveler's Protector

There are numerous risks to traveling. Usually, we think of accidents or trauma as being the most common risks, but microbial infections are by far the most common cause of serious disease and death resulting from traveling.

If an individual travels overseas, the advice is don't eat or drink anything. Yet, who truly follows this advice? Starving to death isn't the answer. Millions of travelers fail to be meticulous. Thus, traveler's misery afflicts tens of millions of Americans every year.

A wide range of infections may be contracted while traveling, and it isn't always from food and drink. The air can transmit disease, as can close contact with individuals. Recently, several individuals were proven to have contracted tuberculosis during air travel. Sitting next to an infected individual may have been the cause, yet, it was also determined that the air filters in some jets are contaminated with the TB bacteria. From an infectious disease viewpoint, flying is seriously dangerous. Always keep your Oreganol handy.

Oil of wild Oreganol is the traveler's savior. Whether in transit or on site, the oil is the answer. It protects the individual from contracting the majority of infections. For optimal results, use it continuously in combination with careful attention to hygiene. Be sure to saturate a tissue and inhale several times while in air transport. Also, use it regularly during hand washing. If food is consumed, be sure to add a drop or two of oil of oregano. Plus, as a traveler's protection take an Oreganol gelcap with every meal. This will prevent food poisoning from striking.

Drinking contaminated water accounts for the vast majority of travelers' infections, although contamination may also result from swimming or bathing in infested water. Bottled water may be the answer, but the question is where does the bottled water come from? A friend of mine, who frequented Europe and the Middle East, reported that more than once she discovered that phony bottled water was on the market. In fact, this individual stumbled accidentally upon a water bottler: a teenager who was pouring river water into bottles and capping it for sale to tourists. When in doubt, add Oreganol to the water. This will be the ideal insurance plan for a tenuous situation.

For travelers there is a special kit to prepare. It is the Oreganol, that is the oil, the Germ-a-Clenz, and the Oregabiotic capsules. The oil is ideal for putting under the tongue and for topical use, the Oregabiotic is the ideal potent pill for taking internally and for protecting the gut, and the Germ-a-Clenz purifies the air and decontaminates the clothes, hands, or other regions. Such a kit is the travelers' guarantee, which will prevent sudden and/or life-threatening illnesses. It will make the trip a pleasant experience. A person could eliminate all risk and save all sorts of misery: just by being prepared.

Chapter Six   # Conclusion

Infectious disease has inflicted such a high degree of human misery that it is beyond description. It is incontestably the world's greatest killer, accounting for tens of millions of deaths yearly. Once, researchers thought that antibiotics were the universal solution and infections would no longer torment humanity. The scientists were wrong. With few exceptions, all of the modern, as well as ancient, infectious diseases seem unstoppable: perhaps they can be driven back at best, but, they merely resurface. Even the most antiquated infections, such as bubonic plague, scarlet fever, whooping cough, diphtheria, and rheumatic fever, are returning.

The immense effects of infectious disease upon our society today is amply illustrated by the fact that some 40,000 to 60,000 North Americans die every year from the flu alone. Think about it; with all the modern facilities and advancements, still this many people are dying from a potentially curable virus?

Disability, disfigurement, and premature death are the expected consequences of the endless litany of incorrigible infectious diseases which continuously afflict humanity such as staph/strep, E. coli., venereal disease, salmonella, cholera, typhus, flesh-eating bacteria, camphylobacter, cholera, dysentery, mycoplasma, Epstein-Barr, HIV, Heliobacter, and herpes. Every day millions of individuals die unnecessarily from infections. The toll inflicted upon humanity is essentially immeasurable. What a travesty it is that much of the essence of the human race is destroyed as a consequence of preventable and curable diseases.

The problem with infections today is that there is no guarantee of medical cure. None of the drugs seem to work anymore. It used to be that basic antibiotics, such as penicillin and sulfa drugs, could be relied upon to eradicate infections or at least those of bacterial origin. Now, these drugs are largely impotent against the majority of bacterial strains. After penicillin's failure, medical doctors relied upon newer and more potent synthetic drugs, but even these are faltering. For topical use medicine offers virtually nothing which can consistently prevent or reverse infections. What's more, the war against viruses is a total failure; there are essentially no drugs which combat them, and over-the-counter medicines at best relieve symptoms and may actually prolong the illness. For instance, anti-fever medicines, such as aspirin and acetaminophen, interfere with the immune response and often exacerbate infections. Aspirin is responsible for its own infectious disease: Reye's syndrome, which is routinely fatal. Non-steroidal anti-inflammatory drugs, such as ibuprofen (Motrin) and Indocin, have recently been implicated with increased risk for yet another killer: flesh-eating bacteria.

Think about it. If you get a cold or flu, what can you do about it? You can't always go to the doctor, and if you do, there is nothing he/she can do about it. Perhaps the physician will feel pressured to prescribe an antibiotic. However, it fails to help, since antibiotics kill only bacteria, and colds/flu are caused by viruses. You are left to soak in your own secretions, tired, miserable, and despondent. Certainly, you might try to combat the virus with any number of "natural" remedies: vitamin C, echinacea, garlic, vinegar, honey, and the like. Yet, nothing seems to place a major dent in the sickness. Enter oregano oil: now there is a substance capable of producing rapid relief if not outright eradication of the various infections caused by cold and flu viruses.

Oil of oregano is one of those rare substances that can alter the course of history. It possesses dependable anti-infective powers; in other words, if a contagious infection develops, oil of oregano is one of the few substances known that will produce consistent positive results.

Oreganol and Oregamax are blanket protection against uncountable disorders, particularly infectious diseases. Infection can strike at any moment, and the unsettling possibilities are immense. Colds, the flu, tonsillitis, hepatitis, tuberculosis, Lyme, strep, staph, Salmonella, Shigella, Listeria, E. coli, typhus, cholera, Candida, Giardia, Cyclospora, Cryptosporidium, dysentery, Herpes, Meningococcus, encephalitic virus, HIV, Ebola, dengue, and Hantavirus can attack virtually anyone, no matter how healthy he/she might be. Currently, E. coli, Listeria, and Salmonella are ravaging the human race. However, any of the aforementioned germs/infections could suddenly strike, causing a local or global epidemic. Rely upon oregano oil, because it saves lives when all else fails. In the event of a severe epidemic affecting thousands or millions, rely also on the edible/researched Oreganol SuperStrength. This high potency wild oregano oil offers the added power needed in a crisis. It can be used repeatedly under the tongue for the most difficult circumstances. In an epidemic for guaranteed protection the secret is to use it frequently, even as often as every five minutes. The results would be astounding, and as a result, thousands, perhaps millions, of lives would be saved. It is dangerous to be ill prepared, because these killers may strike unexpectedly. Not only is it the epitome of misery to contract such a condition, a number of them are rapidly fatal and have no medical cure. No one can afford to take that risk. Why leave home without protection, why enter another country unarmed, and why take risks when a dependable savior is available?

While the degree of disease and disability caused by acute infections is astounding, what is little appreciated is that a wide range of chronic diseases are caused largely by infections. In other words, physicians fail to make the connection between chronic infection and disease. Thus, a variety of diseases which have an infectious component, such as arthritis, cancer, fibromyalgia, lupus, chronic fatigue syndrome, rosacea, gastritis, Crohn's disease, ulcerative colitis, eczema, psoriasis, and peptic ulcer, are never appropriately treated. Antibiotics don't work for these conditions; rather, it is the natural antiseptics as well as nutritional therapy that is the answer.

Medicine is incapacitated by the rising incidence of infectious diseases, particularly drug-resistant infections. Obviously, drugs have failed to protect humanity against the ravages of infectious diseases, since the death rate from infections has risen steadily every decade for the past thirty years. It is evident that only natural antibiotics and antiseptics can be relied upon for salvation. This is because there is no guarantee that if powerful diseases, such as flesh-eating bacteria, cryptosporidium, ebola, dengue, Hantavirus, Lyme, E. coli, Salmonella, hepatitis, encephalitis, or tuberculosis, strike the individual will survive even with the help of modern medicine. The disease might consume the individual without a chance for defense. This illustrates the critical importance of having available the most effective natural medicine, the oil of oregano, to rely upon in the event that serious infection strikes. You truly cannot leave home without it.

Unfortunately, the majority of North Americans have a dangerous attitude. Millions of individuals take it for granted that if an infection strikes, the doctors will take care of it. Such individuals fail to appreciate the seriousness of the infectious epidemics. The fact is if a major infection strikes, there is no guarantee whatsoever that the doctor can save your life. What if the infection is a virus and there are no drugs against it, what if it is a fungus that is immune to the drugs, and what if it is a bacteria that is resistant to the antibiotics? Who will you turn to then? How often it is that a patient contracts a serious infection, especially in hospitals, and nothing can be done to halt the progression. The drugs that are given fail to halt the course, and the patient deteriorates rapidly. The physician, rather, the team of physicians, stand by helplessly, unable to salvage organ, limb, or life. This is senseless, since there are natural medicines which could save the day. Oil of oregano is one such medicine.

It is crucial to understand that not all oregano offers the same degree of anti-infective power. Virtually all of the commercially available compounds are not true oregano at all. Wild oregano, the type which contains measurable antiseptic actions, is difficult to procure. It is a delicate plant which must be specially prepared and processed in order to retain the active components.

The medicinal powers of oregano are found only in a few

species. Beware of poor quality oregano oils, which are made from inferior grade materials or perhaps from plants not even belonging to the oregano species. Beware also of the fact that virtually all of the commercially available oregano oil is not oregano oil. Rather, it is thyme oil, made from the so-called Spanish oregano. Or, it may be marjoram oil, which is a weakling compared to a true oregano oil. Beware also of the cheaper grades of oregano oil with low carvacrol content. The wild oregano oil is an expensive herb to procure, plus it is rather rare. The inexpensive types may be marketed as oil of Origanum vulgare, but these oils are usually not true oregano oil. In fact, Origanum vulgare is a common distinction signifying farm-raised oregano, which is inferior compared to the original wild mountain grown types. The point is the name of the species is unimportant. It is the chemical profile that is critical. Oreganol has the ideal profile, that is P73. This stands for several special types of mountainous oregano which are 100% edible. The P73 wild oregano is the subject of intensive research. The research, performed at Georgetown University, proves that P73 wild high mountain oregano thoroughly destroys germs, including potential human killers like Candida and staph. The P73 Oreganol even killed drug-resistant germs, known as super-germs. What's more, in contrast to all other oregano oils, P73 is a blend, that is it is a rich mixture of several high grade wild oreganos. It is this blending which makes it so unique. What's more, all of the oregano oils in P73 are wild. Herbs that grow in the wild are far more powerful than mere farm-raised herbs. Note: beware of farm-raised oregano products. They may even be genetically engineered. Such cheap imitations may contain inedible components. In other words, they may not be screened for edibility. The Oreganol and Oregamax are 100% edible. Incidentally, because of its quality and dependability, this type of oregano won a special Canadian award for the year 2000 as the number one herbal product.

The advice given in this book applies only to oregano made from the high yield oil species found in various regions throughout the world. The oil and spice are derived from plants grown in virgin soil in clean, chemical-free mountainous areas. Because of its unique properties, no other oregano can be depended upon to elicit the benefits mentioned herein. Farm-raised oregano is simply not the same as the wild, mountain grown type used in Oreganol (P73).

Do not consume commercial, that is undiluted, essential oils of any type internally. With certain essential oils organ toxicity is possible. A number of commercially available essential oils are inedible; caution must be exerted. If you regularly drink alcohol or if you are taking numerous prescription drugs, do not take essential oils internally. Drugs and alcohol cause liver damage, and this disrupts the ability of the liver to process herbs. However, natural crude herbs, like crushed wild oregano, as found in Oregamax, are non-toxic and, thus, may be taken without concern even by individuals taking numerous drugs.

Oil of oregano made from the oil-rich, edible, wild herb is available from North American Herb & Spice Company. The crushed wild herb is made by the same company under the name Oregamax. Both are food-like substances, which may be utilized for health improvement. Unless the maker can certify in writing that the oregano herb or oil is derived from pure, wild edible oregano, avoid consuming it. Be particularly cautious of low priced bottled essential oils promoted as "oregano, marjoram, *Origanum vulgare,* or oregano leaf oil." According to Craker and Vomer's *Herbs, Spices, and Medicinal Plants,* items labeled or promoted as Origanum vulgare are strictly marjoram, that is they are not the true oregano species. These marjoram-source oils lack the active ingredients responsible for oregano oil's useful properties. In fact, marjoram, whether wild or commercial, is regarded by researchers as an "oil poor" species with minimal therapeutic potential. Thus, to achieve the benefits described in this book use Oreganol or Oregacyn (P73) oil of oregano by North American Herb & Spice, as this is certified as edible oregano oil. What's more, it is guaranteed wild, plus it is the subject of modern research. It is produced by steam distillation without the use of chemicals or solvents. Note: this degree of quality is only found in two other brands: Physician's Strength and Oreganum. These products contain the original P73 wild oregano oil blend. This is a special blend of the oils of several species of wild oregano. The key is it is a blend. This makes it more sophisticated, as well as more potent, than any other type. Look for P73 on the label. It is the assurance of quality, research, safety, and efficacy. This is the original edible oregano product developed for human use. If the label fails to list P73, it is not the original high mountain and wild oregano, the type researched at Georgetown University. Oregamax is another important brand to recognize. This is the original crude wild oregano formula. This formula has been successfully used by millions of individuals as well as animals. Oregacyn is a third type of wild oregano product. This is a blend of several spice extracts. It contains the P73 wild oregano blend as well as additional antiseptic spice extracts, including cumin and sage extracts. Avoid cheap fakes and imitations. The point is North American Herb & Spice created the entire wild oregano business. They are the experts. I exclusively use and recommend their products.

If you have a concern about using the oil internally, rub it on the skin, as this will provide benefits. The aroma alone is invigorating. However, be reassured that oil of wild oregano made from the edible mountainous spice is highly safe, because it is made from a natural food. Thus, it is safer to consume than many commercial items, like artificially sweetened pop, which contains the synthetic sweetener, aspartame, or deep fried foods, which contain partially synthetic fat, that is hydrogenated oils.

Oregano oil is a safe but potent substance. Only small amounts are needed to create the desired response. Rubbed on the skin it is safe in rather large amounts, although, again, usually only modest amounts are required. However, for stubborn conditions it may be necessary to use large amounts on the skin. For sensitive skin the oil should be diluted in a fatty medium such as olive oil, cocoa butter, lanolin, or coconut oil. Taken internally, it is active in tiny amounts.

When an individual develops an illness, he/she often becomes desperate, and this is understandable. Oil of oregano is such a godsend that many individuals might think that more is better. In some cases this may be true. A good example is someone who has a cold or flu. It may be necessary to take several drops on the hour until the symptoms abate. However, initially use it as recommended; take small amounts, like a few drops daily. If it is a stubborn condition which fails to respond, take more, like double or triple the recommended amount. Remember, in high doses essential oils are toxic. The body can metabolize small amounts, so hold to the recommendations in this book. However, it is reassuring to know that millions of individuals have used the oil with no ill effects, rather, with deliberate, measurable positive results. In other words, the original emulsified oil of wild oregano is an exceptionally safe herbal medicine. Plus, the oil of wild oregano is a food grade oil more than a true essential oil. The crushed wild herb, the Oregamax, is completely safe for all ages. Thus, for those who are concerned about possible interactions, take the Oregamax as a safe herbal tonic, a few capsules daily. Oregamax is completely safe for all ages as well as pregnant women. There is one area of caution, that is people on multiple medications, especially those with cardiac disorders should proceed with caution. This is because oil of wild oregano is a positive ionotrope, that is it strengthens the pumping power of the heart. In such cases see your doctor before introducing any new therapy. Even so, oil of oregano is a tremendously potent spice extract which is beneficial to cardiac function. Oregano was used by the ancient Greeks to strengthen the function of the heart. It increases the ability of the heart to pump blood. Thus, for those with sensitive systems who are taking blood pressure medication, be aware that the oil is spicy and potent. Take only a small amount, like a drop daily in a glass of water. Or, introduce the oil by adding a single drop in a glass of water. Another method is to introduce the oil by adding a single drop to a tablespoon of extra virgin olive oil. It is well tolerated in these administrations. The point is that the edible oil of wild oregano, that is the Oregacyn and Oreganol P73, is a potent natural substance. Use the least amount necessary. Despite caution or concern there is a simple fact about the potential for side effects: the usual effect is that the individual experiences an improvement of health even in unexpected areas. In other words, illnesses and symptoms disappear. Energy, strength, stamina, and immune capacity improve. Untoward effects are rare. There are no deaths or serious illnesses on record from these substances. However, there are two possible side effects. One of these is constipation, which occurs if excess amounts of the oil are consumed. This is because the oil is an antiseptic, and it may kill a certain amount of the healthy bacteria. Interestingly, raw garlic also kills healthy bacteria. If this occurs, it is advisable to take a healthy bacteria supplement. This may be taken at night or at a time when not taking the oregano oil. Oregamax is more gentle and fails to cause the same type of reaction. The other possible side effect is a temporary rise in blood pressure. All spices can temporarily raise blood pressure, yet incredibly, when taken consistently, they cause the blood pressure to normalize. Thus in numerous human cases, the oil, and the Oregamax, have reverse blood pressure disorders.

Oregacyn is a new, unique product that is the state-of-the-art in wild oregano/spice extracts. Made from various wild and mountain-grown spice extracts, it is available in three easy-to-use forms; capsules, gelcaps, and oil. Oregacyn is particularly valuable for respiratory conditions, especially asthma, bronchitis, and sinusitis. It is also invaluable for bacterial overgrowth. Recently, it was used successfully by a hospitalized diabetic patient diagonosed with cellulitis. About to lose his foot to an amputation, high doses of Oregacyn were used. He was released from the hospital completely healthy and with his foot intact.

Recently, a scientific study was performed on Oregacyn. The Oregacyn, when introduced to the human coronavirus in vitro, completely destroyed this virus after only twenty minutes of exposure. The coronavirus is the microbe responsible for nearly 50% of the infections diagnosed as the common cold or pneumonia and is solely responsible for SARS (Severe Acute Respiratory Syndrome). With studies such as this which demonstrate the tremendous benefits of Oregacyn P73, everyone should have a bottle of it in their cupboard.

As I close this book I received a call from a young gentleman, who told me a story that touched my heart. This 32-year-old was previously debilitated with a severe case of internal fungal infection caused apparently by Candida albicans. His life was essentially destroyed. He was depressed, confused, and lived in a virtual mental fog. His memory was in disarray, and he was unable to work. Despite sleeping most of the day, he was still exhausted. A friend sent him a bottle of oil of oregano and a bottle of Oregamax, which he took rigorously. Today, he informed me that virtually all of his symptoms have disappeared, and he is beginning a new trek: a life free of misery and disease.

Appendix A
Conditions for which oil of oregano may be useful
(listed by body region)

Head and Neck

Dandruff
Seborrhea
Ringworm
Furunculosis
Mastoiditis
Ear infections
Head lice
Cradle cap
Sore throat
Headache
Tonsillitis
Laryngitis

Mouth

Canker sores
Cold sores
Coated tongue
Pyorrhea
Cavities
Lichen planus
Leukoplakia
Thrush
Toothache
Tooth abscess

Respiratory

Bronchitis
Sinusitis
Croup
Pneumonia
Colds
Sore throat
Asthma
Rhinitis
Laryngitis
Emphysema

Digestive

Colitis
Crohn's disease
Diverticulitis
Peptic ulcer
Gastritis
Esophagitis
Flatulence
Hepatitis
Diarrhea
Hiatal hernia

Face

Acne
Sinusitis
Rosacea
Blackheads
Nasal polyps
Folliculitis
Impetigo
Erysipelas
Rhinitis
Trigeminal Neuralgia

Feet

Toenail fungus
Athlete's foot
Calluses/Corns
Ingrown toenail
Bromidrosis

Skin
Acne
Eczema
Psoriasis
Ringworm
Burns
Boils
Cuts and scrapes
Abrasions
Puncture wounds
Flea bites
Allergic rash
Bed sores
Varicose ulcers
Surgical incisions
Itchy skin
Scabies
Pilonidal cysts
Impetigo/Erysipelas
Cellulitis
Dermatitis
Warts
Poison ivy, oak, and sumac
Bee stings/spider bites
Snakebites
Frostbite/frostburn
Animal bites
Bruises
Vitiligo

Musculoskeletal
Arthritis
Sprains
Torn or pulled muscles
Tendonitis
Bursitis
Neuritis
Back strain
Headache
Gout

Genitals and Urinary tract
(Warning: do not apply directly)
Boils
Jock itch
Cystitis
Kidney infection
Scabies
Genital warts

Hands
Hangnails (infected)
Fingernail fungus
Paronychia (infection of the skin surrounding the nail)

Appendix B

Table I Fungal infections against which oregano essential oil may be effective

Aspergillus (aspergillosis)
Blastomycoses
Histoplasmosis
Coccidiomycoses
Cryptococcal infection

Ringworm
Athlete's foot
Nocardiosis
Candida albicans

Table II Bacterial infections against which oregano essential oil may be effective

Actinomycosis
Ehrlichiosis
E. coli
Salmonella
Shigella
Camphylobacter
Enterobacter
Typhoid fever
Cholera
Chlamydia
Strep infection
Staph infection
Tuberculosis
Listeria

Cellulitis
Erysipelas
Pelvic inflammatory disease
Klebsiella
Pseudomonas
Meningitis
Cat scratch fever
Rocky Mountain Spotted Fever
Gonorrhea
Diphtheria
Hemophilus influenza
Lyme disease
Gonorrhea
Pseudomonas

Table III Parasitic diseases against which oregano essential oil may prove effective

Amebic dysentery	Balantidiasis
Cryptosporidium	Giardiasis
Toxoplasmosis	Hookworm
Intestinal flukes	Filariasis
Liver flukes	Lung flukes
Sleeping Sickness	Malaria
Pinworm	Roundworm (aseariasis)
Tapeworms	Trichomonas
Echinococcus (dog tapeworm)	Shistosomiasis

Table IV Viral infections against which oregano essential oil may prove helpful

Colds	Flu
Pneumonia	Croup
Shingles	Cold sores
Measles	Mumps
Warts	Chicken pox
Hantavirus	Herpes
Encephalitis (including West Nile)	

Table V Organisms destroyed by oregano essential oil (as determined by in vitro testing)

Aspergillus flavus	Aspergillus niger
Aspergillus parasiticus	Candida albicans

Camphylobacter jejuni
Bacillus subtilis
Escherichia coli
Pseudomonas aeruginosa
Shigella sonnei
Trichophyton concentricum
Trichophyton mentagrophtes

Giardia lamblia
Staphylococcus aureus
Staphylococcus pre
Salmonella typhi
Helicobacter pylori
Trichophyton rubrum

Table VI Various compounds found in oregano essential oil

Nonane
decane
methyl-2-methylbutyrate
pinene
camphene
hexanal
undecane
sabinene
carene
myrcene
terpinene
limonene
cineole
phellandrene
hexenal
amyl furan
ocimene

cymene
terpinolene
nonanal
linalool
cis-sabinene hydrate
linalyl acetate
terpinen-4-ol
beta-caryophyllene
methyl carvacrol
trans-dihydrocarvone
cis-dihydrocarvone
alpha-humulene
germacrene D
beta-bisabolene
spathcoulane
thymol
carvacrol

Bibliography

Asman, B.J. and P. Fireman. 1988. The role of allergies in the development of otitis media with effusion. *Intl Ped.* 3:231-33.

Azzouz, M.A. and L. B. Bullerman. 1982. Comparative antimycotic effects of selected herbs, spices, plant components, and commercial antifungal agents. *J. Food Protect.* 45:1298.

Bankhead, C. 1996. Food poisoning traced to alfalfa sprouts, lettuce. *Medical Tribune.* Vol. 37, pp. 1,6.

Bellanti, J.A. 1978. *Immunology II.* Philadelphia: W. B. Saunders Co.

Beraoud, L., et al. 1991. Chemical composition of the essential oils of selected plant materials used in Moroccan cuisine. *Al-Birunya, Rev. Mor. Pharm.* 7:49-69.

Brenness, Lesley. 1994. *Herbs, an Eyewitness Handbook.* London: Dorling Kindersley.

Buchanan, R. and F. Tenenbaum (eds). *Taylor's Guide to Herbs.* Boston: Houghton Mifflin Co.

Buchanan, R.L. and A.J. Shepherd. 1981. Inhibition of Aspergillus parasiticus by thymol. *J. Food Sci.* 46:876-977.
Calpouzos, L. 1954. Botanical aspects of oregano. *Econ. Bot.* 8:222-223.

Carroll, John A. 1996. Common Bacterial Pyodermas. *Postgraduate Medicine.* Sept., 100:311-19.

Castleman, M. 1991. *The Healing Herbs.* Emmaus, PA: Rodale Press.

Conner, D.E. and L.R. Beuchat. 1984. Effects of essential oils from plants on growth of food spoilage yeasts. *J. Food Sci.* 49:429.

Craker, L.E. and E. Vomer (eds). 1986. *Herbs, Spices, and Medicinal Plants: Recent Advances in Botany, Horticulture, and Pharmacology.* Vol. 1. New York: Food Products Press (imprint of the Haworth Press, Inc.)

Dayal, B., et al. 1971. Screening of some Indian essential oils for their antifungal properties. *Flav. Ind.* 2:484.

Diamant, M. and B. Diamant. 1974. Abuse and timing of the use of antibiotics in acute otitis media. *Arch. Otolaryngol.* 100:226.

The Editors. 1996. Rosacea linked to Demodex organisms. *Family Practice News.* Sept. 15.

Farrell, K. 1985. *Spices, Condiments, and Seasonings.* Westport, CT: AVI Publ. Co.

Gerard's Herball (from the edition of T.H. Johnson, 1636. 1964. London: Spring Books.

Grieve, M. 1971. *A Modern Herbal.* New York: Dover Publications

Hitokoto, H., et al. 1980. Inhibitory effects of spices on growth and toxin production of toxgienic fungi. *Appl. Envir. Micro.* 39:818.

Hussar, A. E. and H. L. Holley. 1954. *Antibiotics and Antibiotic Therapy.* New York: Macmillan Co.

Ingram, Cass. 1989. *Eat Right to Live Long.* Cedar Rapids, IA: Knowledge House.

Ingram, Cass. 1992. *Killed on Contact: The Tea Tree Oil Story, Nature's Finest Antiseptic.* Cedar Rapids, IA: Knowledge House.

Ingram, Cass. 1994. *How to Survive Disasters with Natural Medicines.* Cedar Rapids, IA: Knowledge House.

Ingram, Cass. 1994. *Self-Test Nutrition Guide*. Cedar Rapids, IA: Knowledge House.

Ietswaart, J.H. 1980. *A taxonomic revision of the genus Origanum* (Labiatae. Leiden) The Hague: University Press, pp. 1523.

Janssen, A.M., et al. 1987. Antimicrobial activities of essential oils. A 1976-1986 literature review on possible applications. *Pharm Week bl.* 9:193-97.

Jerome, F. 1995. *Tooth Truth*. San Diego: Promotion Publishing.

Johnson, D.A. 1996. Heliobacter pylori and GI disease. *Consultant*, Sept., pp. 1911-12.

Kurita, N., et al. 1979. Antifungal activity and molecular orbical energies of aldehyde compounds from oils of higher plants. *Agric. Biol. Chem.* 43:2365-71.

Kurita, N. and S. Koike. 1982. Synergistic antimicrobial effect of an acetic acid, sodium chloride, and essential oil components. *Agric. Biol. Chem.* 46:1655-60.

Lamaison, J.L., et al. 1991. Lamiacees medicinales a proprieties antioxydantes, sources potentielles d'acide rosmarinique. *Pharm. Acta Helv.* 66:185-88.

Lawrence, B. M. 1984. The botanical and chemical aspects of oregano. *Perf. Flav.* 9:41-51.

Masada, Y. 1975. *Analysis of Essential Oils by GC/MS*. Tokyo: Hirokawa Publ. Co., Inc.

Miloradovich, M. 1952. *The Home and Garden Book of Herbs and Spices*. New York: Doubleday.

Mirelman, D., et al. 1987. Inhibition of the growth of *Entamoeba histolytica* by allicin, the active principle of garlic extract *(Allium sativum)*. *J. Infect. Dis.* 150:243.

Nara Simha, R. and P. Subbarao. 1972. The efficacy of some essential oils on pathogenic fungi. *Flav. Ind.* 3:368.

Parry, J.W. 1953. *The Story of Spices.* New York: Chemical Publ. Co, Inc. pp 11, 58.

Pahlow, Manfried. no date. *Healing Herbs.* New York Botanical Garden: Barron's.

Ponce-Macotela, M., et al. 1994. In vitro antigiardiasic activity of plant extracts. *Rev. Invest. Clin.* 46:343 (abstract in English).

Pruthi, J.S. 1980. *Spices and Condiments: Chemistry, Microbiology, Technology.* New York: Academic Press.

Rinear, C.E. 1986. *The Sexually Transmitted Diseases.* McFarland & Co.

Rizzi-Fischer, Susanne. 1990. *Complete Aromatherapy Handbook: Essential Oils for Radiant Health.* New York: Sterling Publ. Co., Inc.

Rosenburg, E. and P. Belew. 1982. Microbial factors in psoriasis. *Arch. Derm.* 118:1434-44.

Sauer, G. C. 1980. *Manual of Skin Diseases.* (4th ed) Phil: J. P. Lippincott.

Schmidt, M.A. *Childhood Ear Infections.* Berkeley: North Atlantic Books.

Shelef, L.A. 1983. Antimicrobial effects of spices. *J. Food Safety.* 6:29.

Srinivas, S.R. 1986. *Atlas of Essential Oils.* New York: Anadams.

Svendsen, A. B. and J.J.C. Scheffer (eds). 1985. *Essential Oils and Aromatic Plants.* Dordrecht: Martinus Nijhoff/Dr. W. Junk Publ.

Tantaoui-Elaraki, A., et al. 1992. Antimicrobial activity of four chemically different essential oils. *Riv. Ital.* E.P.P.O.S. 6:13-23.

Taintu, D.R. and A.T. Grenis. 1993. *Spices and Seasonings: A Food Technology Handbook.* New York: VCH Publ.

Tetenyi, P. 1970. Infraspecific chemical taxa of medicinal plants. *Akademiai Kiado, Budapest*, pp. 225.

Thomas, C.L. 1981. *Taber's Cyclopedic Medical Dictionary.* Philadelphia: F.A. Davis.

Tucker, A.O. 1981. Which is the true Oregano? *Horticulture.* 59(7):57-59.

Van Buchem, F.L. 1981. Therapy of acute otitis media: myringotomy, antibiotics, or neither? A double-blind study in children. *Lancet,* Oct. 24. Vol. 883.

Wing, Lucy. 1995. Oregano (Recipes from Lucy's Country Garden). *Country Living.* June, Vol. 18:145-53.

Index

A

Achlorhydria, 105
Acne, 41-43, 190, 191
AIDS, 95, 128
Alcohol, 26, 27, 38, 39, 52, 53, 64, 65, 68, 83, 94, 100, 136, 149, 160, 183
  toxicity of, 27, 39
  in mouth washes, 52, 53
Allergic rashes. *See* Rashes
Allergic reactions, 20, 48, 78, 97, 108, 112, 120, 132
Allergies, 80, 162, 163, 158, 159
Ameba, 17, 76
Amebic dysentery, 6, 192
  see also dysentery
Aminoglycosides, 8
Animal bites, 44, 190
Antibiotics, 6-11, 16, 27, 54-60, 77-79, 88, 95, 99, 122, 130, 180
  allergic reactions to, 7
  microbial resistance to, 7, 8, 88, 181
  toxicity of, 11, 79, 122
Antiinflammatory drugs, 27, 46, 176
Antioxidants, 38, 40
Antiseptics, 7, 10, 11, 17, 21, 22, 38, 56, 59, 82, 100, 136, 139, 148, 180
Arbovirus, 80
Arsenic, 10
Arthritis, 34, 46, 47, 86, 126, 17, 187,
Aspergillus, 60
Asthma, 81, 86, 187
Athlete's foot, 24, 83, 123, 157, 169, 190, 192
Athletic injuries, 123, 124

Atopy, 81
Attention deficit syndrome, 79, 86

B

Bacillus subtilis, 194
Bacterial infection, 55, 58, 76, 78, 82, 108, 124, 192
  see also individual infections
Bad breath, 52, 53
Balantidiasis, 192
Bed sores, 53, 54, 191
Bee stings, 98, 190
Beta carotene, 38
Bioflavonoids, 88
  see also Flavonoids
Biotin, 74
Birch oil, 20
Birth control pills, 27, 28, 65, 95
Bites, 33, 44, 80, 126, 132, 152, 191
  see also Animal bites; Dog bites
Bladder infection, 55, 156
Blastomycoses, 190
Boils, 57-59, 190
Bone marrow, 8, 27, 65
Bromidrosis, 57, 192
Bronchitis, 34, 60, 61, 190
Bruises, 61, 62, 123, 191
Burns, 62, 63, 113, 191
Bursitis, 64, 65, 191

C

Calcium, 36, 37, 64, 68, 89, 100, 101, 129, 145, 163
Calcium deposits, 64
Camphylobacter, 76, 192

see also Helicobacter
Cancer, 5, 6, 39, 54, 71, 125, 164, 170, 180
   skin, 164
   stomach, 125
Candida albicans, 23, 29, 43, 56, 59, 65, 74, 76, 79, 83, 104, 111, 113, 127, 192
Candidiasis, 65
Canker sores, 66, 67, 190
Carbolic acid, 21, 22, 39
Cardiomyopathy, 27, 126
Carvacrol, 18, 21-23, 39, 56
Cat scratch fever, 192
Cavities, 94, 120, 190
Cephalosporins, 7
Chemotherapeutic agents, 27
Chicken pox, 68, 118, 193
   see also Herpes
Chlamydia, 111, 192
Chlorophyll, 57
Clostridium, 76
Clove, 10, 20, 21, 57
Coccidiomycoses, 192
Cold sores, 68, 190
   see also Herpes; Chicken pox
Colds, 35, 49, 68-70, 168, 178, 179, 190, 193
Coriander, 10, 17, 20
Corns, 187
Cortisone, 28, 50, 68, 82, 98, 119
Cough, 9, 13, 35, 49, 60, 61, 70, 71, 106, 155, 156, 162,, 163, 177
Cradle cap, 187
Croup, 190
Cryptosporidium, 72, 76, 179, 180, 193
Cuts, 124, 192
Cyclospora, 140, 176, 179
Cystitis, 192

D
Dandruff, 72-74, 190
Deer tick, 126
   see also Ticks; Tick-borne illnesses; Lyme disease
Demodex, 115
Dengue fever, 80
Dermatitis, 192
Dermatophytes, 23, 50-52, 83
   see also Fungal infection; Tinea
Diabetes, 5, 54
Diabetic foot ulcers, 55
Diaper rash, 74, 75
Diarrhea, 76, 77, 86, 90, 154, 156, 157, 190
Dog bites, 45
   see also Animal bites
Dysentery, 6, 74, 141, 175, 179, 193
   see also Amebic dysentery

E
E. coli, 16, 23, 42, 56, 76, 77, 140, 141, 177, 179, 180, 192
Earaches, 70
Ear infections, 76-79, 190
Ebola, 80, 179, 180
Echinococcus, 193
Eczema, 80-82, 86, 192
Encephalitis, 126, 168, 193
Enterobacter, 76, 192
Ehrlichiosis, 124, 192
Erysipelas, 67, 190-193
Erythromycin, 8
Escherichia coli. *See* E. coli
Essential fatty acids, 47, 59, 74, 78, 81
Essential oils, 10, 18-21, 23, 71, 91, 101, 103, 134, 183 184, 186

F

Fiber, 100
Fibromyalgia, 86, 126, 180
Filariasis, 190
Fingernail fungus, 80, 83, 191
Flavonoids, 39
Flea bites, 191
Flesh-eating bacteria, 137, 175, 178
Flu, 5, 6, 35, 48, 68-70, 76, 82, 150, 152, 155, 168, 177-179, 184, 193
Flukes, 76, 193
Folic acid, 46, 59, 60, 78, 81, 89, 100, 114
Food poisoning, 76, 77, 88-90, 140, 141, 168, 173
Frostbite/Frostburn, 85, 191
Frozen shoulder syndrome, 64, 65
Fungal infections, 25-29, 74, 97, 103, 192

G

Gallic acid, 101, 148
Gangrene, 55
Gastritis, 178, 190
Genital warts, 191
Giardia lamblia, 85, 193
Giardiasis, 85, 86, 168, 193
Goldenseal, 10, 57
Gonorrhea, 111, 192
Gout, 20, 191
Grape, sour. *See* Sour Grape
Gum disease, 88

H

Halitosis. *See* Bad breath
Hand washing technique, 75, 144, 167
Hantavirus, 179, 180
Head lice. *See* Lice

Headache, 33, 35, 86, 92-94, 126, 191
Hearing Loss, 151
Helicobacter pylori, 104, 105, 116, 125, 194
Hemlock, poison, 33
Hemophilus influenza, 192
Hemorrhagic fever. *See* Ebola; Dengue fever
Hepatitis, 6, 8, 75, 86, 94-96, 112, 126, 168, 179, 180
Herpes, 68, 69, 118, 122, 157, 177, 179, 193
see also Cold sores; Shingles
Hexachlorophene, 136
Hiatal hernia, 190
High blood pressure, 27
Hippocrates, 149
Histoplasmosis, 192
Hives. *See* Rash
Hookworm, 76, 193
Hormones, 43
see also Adrenal glands; Thyroid gland
Hydrogen peroxide, 136
Hygiene, 66, 75, 83, 90, 104, 110, 117, 144, 167, 168, 173

I

Ingram, Dr. Cass, 49, 74
Impetigo, 68, 98, 99, 192
Influenza. *See* Flu
Insecticides, 112
Iodine, 10, 136
Iron, 36, 37
Irritable bowel syndrome, 86, 98, 100
Itchy skin, 112, 192
see also Rash

J-K

Jock itch, 123, 192
Klebsiella, 56, 193
Kidney infection, 191
Killer bees, 132
    see also Bee stings

L

Lactobacillus acidophilus, 8, 100
Laryngitis, 190
Lawless, Julia, 16, 18
Leaky gut syndrome, 86
Leg cramps, 102
Leukoplakia, 190
Lice, 90, 91, 190
Lichen planus, 190
Lindane, 118
Liver, 8, 20, 26, 29, 37, 38, 44, 50-
    52, 72, 86, 87, 94-97, 103, 112,
    113, 170, 183
    failure, 8, 112
    see also Hepatitis
Lung infection, 106, 162
    see also Bronchitis; Pneumonia
Lupus, 180
Lyme disease, 125, 126, 180, 178, 192

M

Magnesium, 36, 37, 76, 81, 100, 101,
    129, 145, 163,
Malaria, 190
Malic acid, 101
Manganese, 36
Marjoram, 12, 181
Marjoram oil, 12, 17, 18, 20, 182, 184
Mastoiditis, 190
Measles, 193
Meningitis, 126, 164, 192

Mercury compounds, 10
Mint, 15, 17, 20, 41, 49, 148
Mites, 43, 115-117, 169
    see also Demodex; Scabies
Mold, 25, 61, 93, 94, 120, 163
Mouthwashes
    alcohol content of, 53
Mucopolysaccharides, 47
Mumps, 193
Mycoplasma, 177
    see also Tuberculosis
Mycobacterium tuberculosis, 129
    see also Tuberculosis

N

Nail fungus. *See* Fingernail fungus;
    Toenail fungus
Narcotic poisoning, 33
Nasal polyps, 190
Nausea, 68, 86
Necrotizing fasciitis.
    See Flesh eating bacteria
Neuritis, 123, 126, 160, 192
Niacin, 38, 47

O

Olive oil, 24, 48, 50, 58, 64, 68, 98,
    112, 113, 136
Onion, 20, 21, 57, 107, 161
Origanum vulgare, 17, 182, 184

P

Pantothenic acid, 46, 47, 78, 100, 114
Parasites, 16, 17, 47,, 48, 76, 77, 86, 91,
    106, 150, 158, 171
    see also individual diseases
Paronychia, 103, 104, 191
Pediculosis. *See* Lice

Penicillin, 7, 9, 10, 178
Pennyroyal, 20
Peptic ulcer, 104, 105, 180, 189
pH, 43, 44, 66
Phenol, 10, 21, 22, 37, 39, 41
Pilonidal cyst, 192
Pinworm, 76, 144, 193
Pneumonia, 68, 106, 190
Phosphorus, 36, 89, 145
Plaque, 54
Poison ivy, 107, 152, 191
Poison oak, 107, 191
Poison sumac, 107, 191
Potassium, 36, 38, 76, 100, 101
Prostate, 65, 110, 111
Prostatitis, 110
Protein, 37, 50, 51, 109, 114
Proteus, 56, 111
Pruritis, 112
    see also Itchy skin; Rash
Pseudomonas, 17, 23, 169, 192
Psoriasis, 86, 108, 109, 192
Pyorrhea, 88, 190
    see also Gum disease
Pyridoxine, 81
    see also Vitamin B-6

Q-R
Radiation, 27, 67, 113, 114
Radiation burns, 113, 114
Rash, 35, 44, 74, 75, 79, 99, 107, 108,
    112, 113, 115, 117, 124, 126, 152,
    191
Respiratory diseases, 71, 78, 122, 190
    see also Lung infections;
    individual diseases
Reye's Syndrome, 178

Rhinitis, 190
Rhus coriaria, 101, 148, 161
Riboflavin, 38, 59, 74, 78, 81, 89, 114
Ringworm, 50, 83, 114, 115, 190
Rocky Mountain Spotted Fever, 125, 192
Rosacea, 115, 116, 156, 180
Roundworm, 76, 193

S
Sage, Mexican, 12
Salmonella, 16, 42, 140, 177-180, 194
Scabies, 116-118, 188
Sebaceous glands, 42, 58, 59, 114
    infection of,58, 114
Seborrhea, 73, 74, 160, 190
Selenium, 46, 78, 100, 114
Sepsis, 55, 136
Shigella, 6, 76, 179, 189, 194
Shistosomiasis, 193
Shingles, 118, 193
Seizures, 33, 162
Silver nitrate, 10
Sinus problems, 70, 79, 93, 94, 160,
    161
    see also Sinusitis
Sinusitis, 35, 119, 120, 190
Sleeping sickness, 193
Snake bites, 132
Sore throat, 35, 49, 68, 70, 121, 122,
    190
Spanish oregano, 17, 18, 182
Spleen, 8, 27, 29, 50, 129
Splinters, 158
Sports injuries, 123
Staph, 16, 23, 42, 56, 59, 60, 81, 98,
    99, 104, 111, 122, 137, 177, 179,
    182, 190

Stomachache, 158
Strep, 23, 43, 56, 59, 60, 67, 68, 82,
    98, 99, 104, 122, 137, 177, 190
Sugar, 26, 28, 42, 49, 50, 65, 79, 83,
    88, 103, 109
Sulfa drugs, 7, 178

T
Tannic acid, 101, 148
Tapeworms, 76, 193
Tea tree oil, 19, 20, 151
Tendonitis, 123, 191
Terpenes, 38, 39, 101
Tetracyclines, 7, 8
Thiamine, 38
Thrush, 127, 128
Thyme, 10, 18, 19
Thyme oil, 17-19, 22, 183
Thymol, 18, 22, 194
Thyroid gland, 64
Tick-borne illnesses, 125-127
    see also Lyme disease
Ticks, 125-127
Tinea, 114, 115
Toenail fungus, 52, 190
Tonsillitis, 187
Toothache, 34, 128, 129, 190
Toxoplasmosis, 193
Trace minerals.
    See individual minerals
Trichomonas, 193
Trichophyton, 194
    see also Dermatophytes; Tinea;
    Ringworm; Fungal infection
Tuberculosis, 6, 129, 130, 173, 179,
    180, 192
Typhus, 6, 91, 177, 179

U-V
Ulcers, 47, 53-55, 104, 105, 114,
    125, 191
Vaginal infection, 75
    see also Vaginitis
Vaginitis, 65
Varicose ulcers, 53, 191
Varicose veins, 54, 131
Venomous bites, 33, 132
Viruses, 16, 17, 67, 69, 70, 76, 78,
    95, 106, 121, 122, 143, 155, 178,
    179, 191
Vitamins, 36-38, 46, 81, 114, 159
Vitamin A, 45, 46, 78, 89, 100, 114
Vitamin B. See Niacin
Vitamin B-1. See Thiamine
Vitamin B-2, See Riboflavin
Vitamin B-6, See Pyridoxine
Vitamin B-12, 100,
Vitamin C, 38, 45, 46, 78, 89, 114,
    149, 178
Vitamin D, 46, 89, 100, 114, 129
Vitamin E, 45, 114
Vitamin K, 38, 89, 100

W-Z
Warts, 134, 135, 159, 191
White blood cells, 9, 27, 29, 44, 80
Wounds, 33, 44, 54, 80, 85, 113, 114,
    123, 135, 136, 171, 191
Yeast infection, 25, 65, 121, 127
    see also Candida albicans;
    Fungal infection
Zinc, 35, 37, 45, 58, 59, 74, 81, 101,
    114

Books and Cassettes

#1 *How to Eat Right and Live Longer*—$21.95
373 pages   6 x 9 inch softbound   ISBN 0911119213
Dr. Ingram's most comprehensive book on diet and nutrition. Describes the treatment of a wide range of illnesses through diet and nutritional supplementation. Emphasis is on the nutritional treatment of heart disease, high cholesterol, high triglycerides, diabetes, obesity, allergies, arthritis, neurological disorders, and alcoholism. Step-by-step nutritional protocols, dietary instruction, personalized nutritional/blood analysis, and 100 recipes included.

#2 *Nutrition Tests for Better Health*—$24.95
374 pages   5 1/2 x 8 1/2 inch softbound   ISBN 1931078084
Test yourself to determine your nutritional deficiencies from *A to zinc*. Other tests show evidence of possible health problems such as adrenal insufficiency, chemical toxicity, thyroid insufficiency, intestinal malabsorption, liver dysfunction, and premature aging. Sugar, caffeine, sulfite, food dye, and MSG overload also evaluated. Each test followed by specific and thorough nutritional recommendations. Find out what you are lacking.

#3 *Natural Cures for Headaches*—$19.95
250 pages   5 1/2 x 8 1/2 inch softbound   ISBN 1931078092
A nutritional approach to solving the migraine dilemma. Emphasizes food allergies, nutritional deficiencies, and hormonal disturbances and how to diagnose them as well as how to reverse them nutritionally. Chapter on structural therapy for tension headaches included.

#4 *Tea Tree Oil: The Natural Antiseptic*—$12.95
119 pages   5 1/2 x 8 1/2 inch softbound   ISBN 0911119493
Some things need to be killed: bacteria, viruses, fungi, parasites, and parasitic insects. Learn how to battle infectious disease with tea tree oil, one of Nature's most versatile and potent antiseptics. Information particularly valuable for homemakers, travelers, wilderness buffs, fishermen, and athletes.

#5 *Natural Cures for Killer Germs*—$19.95
348 pages   5 1/2 x 8 1/2 inch softbound   ISBN 1931078106
Dangerous infections can strike at any moment. Protect yourself now with Dr. Ingram's powerful protocols. Sections include candidiasis, mad cow, bird flu, staph, Lyme, encephalitis, mold, parasites, SARS, TB sepsis, AIDS, whopping cough, hepatitis: all can be cured. Protect yourself from epidemics now.

#6 *Supermarket Remedies for Better Health*—$29.95
325 pages   6 1/4 x 9 1/4 inch hardbound   ISBN 0911119647
Reverse health problems with foods, herbs, and spices. Learn to shop for your ailments at the supermarket, health store, and farmer's market. Included among the numerous examples are a supermarket juice that reverses heart disease, a vegetable that halts depression, a berry which eliminates stomach aches, a fruit which lowers cholesterol, a berry for poor vision, a protein for great energy, a spice which kills germs and much more. Use supermarket remedies for hundreds of ailments.

#7 *The Cure is in the Cupboard: How to Use Oregano for Better Health*—$19.95
203 pages–Revised Edition 51/2 x 81/2 inch softback ISBN 0911119744
Oregano helps you regain your health and then stay healthy. This is what saved Dr. Ingram's life. Learn how to use oregano and its essential oil for fighting infection and eliminating pain. Combat skin disorders, injuries, wounds, and dental problems. Particularly valuable for fungal infections.

#8 *Lifesaving Cures*—$19.95
312 pages, 6x 9 inch softback ISBN 1931078009
To survive in the 21st century you must know lifesaving cures. This book describes the most powerful remedies for reversing everyday illnesses. With this book of natural cures Dr. Ingram provides hundreds of natural answers for dozens of ailments.

#9 *The Respiratory Solution*—$14.95
206 pages, 5.5x 8.5 inch softback ISBN 1931078076
Learn the most powerful natural cures for reversing dozens of respiratory ailments. Gain fast relief from sinus problems, allergies, mold, bronchial problems, colds, flu and much more using edible natural foods and herbs.

#10 *The Longevity Solution*—$12.95
144 pages, 5.5x 8.5 inch softback ISBN 1931078017
A book that explains the incredible powers of royal jelly. Reverse fatigue, hormonal problems, hot flashes, anxiety, depression, insomnia, irritability, panic attacks, and much more. Stall the aging process with royal jelly.

Cassette Tapes and Programs

#1 *How to Use Oregano for Common Illnesses*—$9.95
A must for oregano lovers. Contains detailed information not found in the book. Specific protocols for dozens of illnesses and diseases plus case histories. Learn hundreds of uses for wild oregano oil and herb—from the Doctor himself.

#2 *Professional/Advanced Series*—$85.00*
Warning Signs of Nutritional
Deficiency 4 tapes Manual: 100 pages, with Judy Kay Gray, M. S.
Master Dr. Ingram's knowledge about nutritional deficiency and natural medicine. Find out how to discern your specific deficiencies; become proficient in spotting nutritional deficiencies in others. Includes lifesaving information on the treatment of disease with nutritional medicine. Become an expert.

#3 *Wild Oregano, Lifesaving Spice*—$9.95
Dr. Ingram's famous lecture on the power of wild oregano. Learn all the most compelling facts—why it works, the research, and true life stories—informative and entertaining.

For ordering information call (800) 243-5242 or for overseas orders call (847) 473-4700. To send a fax: (847) 473-4780. E-mail: droregano@aol.com
For more information about the products mentioned in this book see the Web site, www.Oreganol.com.

ORDER FORM

Item	Quantity	Amount
Books		
Book #1 *How to Eat Right and Live Longer*	————	————
Book #2 *Nutrition Tests for Better Health*	————	————
Book #3 *Who Needs Headaches?*	————	————
Book #4 *Tea Tree Oil: The Natural Antiseptic*	————	————
Book #5 *Natural Cures for Killer Germs*	————	————
Book #6 *Supermarket Remedies*		
Book #7 *The Cure is in the Cupboard*	————	————
Book #8 *Lifesaving Cures*	————	————
Book #9 *The Respiratory Solution*	————	————
Book #10 *The Longevity Solution*	————	————
Cassette Tapes and Programs		
Tape #1 *How to Use Oregano for Common Illnesses*	————	————
Tape #2 *Professional Series* (tapes and manual)	————	————
Tape #3 *Wild Oregano, Lifesaving Spice*	————	————
Sub-Total		————
Sales Tax (if any)		————
Shipping*		————
TOTAL		————

*Shipping Charges: $5.00 for single books—add $1.00 for each additional book. Cassette tape series add $4.00. Payment by check, money order, or credit card.

Make checks payable to: NAHS P.O. Box 4885 Buffalo Grove, IL 60089
telephone: (800) 243-5242

Use the following for VISA, Mastercard or American Express orders:

Credit Card # _____ Exp. Date _____

Name _____

Address _____

City _____ State _____ Zip_____